the
Holy Bible
of
Inclusion

D.E. Paulk

All scripture quotations are arranged throughout the book in italics and individually referenced by translation.

You may contact D.E. Paulk at:
Cathedral of the Holy Spirit
P.O. Box 371289
Decatur, GA 30037
(404) 243-5020
info@mycathedral.org
www.mycathedral.org
www.pro-love.org
www.weeklyeureka.org

Other books by D.E. Paulk:
I Don't Know... The Way of Knowing
Destroying Religion... Establishing The Kingdom
Finding Sacred in the Secular

D.E. Paulk's Bio

D.E. Paulk is the Senior Pastor of the Cathedral of the Holy Spirit in Atlanta, GA (a thriving multicultural, interfaith, LGBT affirming congregation). D. E. is widely known as a radically inclusive minister of reconciliation who believes that the Christ Spirit is present in all of creation and cannot be defined by, nor confined to, Christianity.

> "Descended from generations of Southern preachers, Donnie Earl is now a preacher himself, though a different breed..." ~Katherine Marsh from the article "Son of a Preacher Man," Rolling Stone Magazine

> "Donnie Earl is progressive... young... hip..." ~Mara Shalhoup from the article "The Young Shepherd," Creative Loafing

His family founded Chapel Hill Harvester Church, now known as The Cathedral of the Holy Spirit (www.mycathedral.org), in 1960. The Paulks have always been known for their ministry of restoration. For over 50 years, the Cathedral has opened its doors to people from every walk of life. This has served as the foundation of who D.E. is today.

D.E. Paulk not only serves as Senior Pastor of The Cathedral of the Holy Spirit, he is also the founder of the Pro-Love Organization (www.pro-love.org) which is an inclusive initiative purposed to bring people of all faiths, cultures and backgrounds together. The Pro-Love Organization hosts a yearly march in the city of Atlanta that unites: Jew and Muslim, Gay and Straight, Atheist and Christian, and all others... D.E. believes the Pro-Love Movement is part of the continuation of Dr. Martin Luther King Jr.'s dream.

Paulk holds a Bachelor of Theology degree and has been the recipient of numerous community, civic and service awards. In 2008, D.E. was inducted into the Morehouse College Dr. Martin Luther King, Jr. International Board of Preachers. In 2009, he was honored by

Cornerstone University in Lake Charles, Louisiana with an honorary doctorate degree for his in-depth theological research and writings. In 2010, D. E. began serving as a National Board Member for the Southern Christian Leadership Conference (S.C.L.C.), the historic civil rights organization founded by Dr. Martin Luther King, Jr. He has authored several books including Finding Sacred in the Secular, Destroying Religion... Establishing the Kingdom, Looking for Dad, and his most recent release entitled I Don't Know... The Way of Knowing.

D.E. Paulk makes his home in suburban Atlanta along with his wife, Brandi, and two children, Esther and Micah.

DEDICATION

I dedicate this book to my children, Esther and Micah. I will never truly be able to accurately explain how unlimited, unconditional and undying my love is for you. There really are no words that would ever suffice. There is nothing you could do that would cause me to not love you. As you begin to understand your earthly father's love you will also embark on embracing the love of your heavenly Father, which is immeasurably greater than mine. As your humanity grows into your divinity; as your mortal surrenders to your immortality; and as you wrestle with eternal truth in this temporary dimension, remember to...

Be bold and courageous. Your love will always conquer your fear.

Love yourself. Approving of you is the only affirmation you will ever need.

Honor your own truth. Remember that truth is a journey, not a destination.

Lend your strength to those in need. Speak for those whose voices have been silenced.

And, never be afraid to take the path less traveled. It will make all the difference.

I love you,

Dad

And who is he who will harm you if you become followers of what is good? But even if you should suffer for righteousness' sake, you are blessed. "And do not be afraid of their threats, nor be troubled." But sanctify the Lord God in your hearts, and always ***BE READY TO GIVE A DEFENSE TO EVERYONE WHO ASKS YOU A REASON FOR THE HOPE THAT IS IN YOU****, with meekness and fear; having a good conscience, that when they defame you as evildoers, those who revile your good conduct in Christ may be ashamed. For it is better, if it is the will of God, to suffer for doing good than for doing evil.*
I Peter 3:13-17 NKJV

———————◆———————

SPECIAL RECOGNITION

To Dr. Harold Lovelace... a precious soul who has labored for more than fifty years to enlighten the Body of Christ to a clearer understanding of the Finished Work of Grace. Dr. Lovelace has traveled near and far to share the Gospel of Good News (that man has been reconciled to God through Christ). All of your spiritual kids are keenly aware that we are standing on the shoulders of a giant. I honor you Dr. Harold Lovelace. You will always be *The Godfather of Inclusion!*

I would also like to say to my cousin, Bishop Jim Swilley... your intense love of, and study in, the Word of God has offered to me an endless reservoir of inspiration, revelation, confirmation, and at times, even affirmation. To discover that Spirit revealed the same truth to you as it did me, both comforted me and allowed me to feel sane again. The babe of revelation living within me leaps up whenever we are together! Your courageous, exhaustive and timeless work, *School of the Bible*, served as a great catalyst and resource for the writing of this book. I honor the gift in you Jamal. Love, Darnell.

THANKS

To my wife, Brandin Paulk; to my sister, LaDonna Paulk Diaz; to the staff, members and faithful supporters of the mission, message and mandate of the Cathedral of the Holy Spirit... thanks for your love, patience, support, expertise and for continuing to take the daily journey toward greater revelation.

And, to my parents, Don and Clariece Paulk... for raising me in an environment of love, tolerance and openness. I always had more than enough oxygen and space to grow and to become.

In his book, *THE HOLY BIBLE OF INCLUSION*, Pastor D. E. Paulk does a much more thorough and comprehensive job of probing the critical concepts of *Inclusion* than I do in my book, *THE GOSPEL OF INCLUSION*. The delicate theological, scriptural and spiritual balance my friend D. E. Paulk walks and writes in this book, is an artistic, tactful and tasteful treatment of some of the most sensitive aspects of both modern and ancient religious doctrine, dogma and discipline.

The subject of *Inclusion* deals more with being and feeling spiritually and mentally *safe* than being and feeling religiously *saved*. I am proud of the expanded consciousness this book embraces and embarks upon in further discussion. During this journey you will inevitably enjoy renewing and re-knowing God (and yourself) all over again - or perhaps for the first time.

Peace is possible.

~ Bishop Carlton D. Pearson

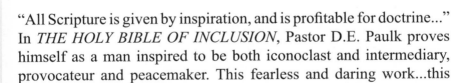

"All Scripture is given by inspiration, and is profitable for doctrine..." In *THE HOLY BIBLE OF INCLUSION*, Pastor D.E. Paulk proves himself as a man inspired to be both iconoclast and intermediary, provocateur and peacemaker. This fearless and daring work...this labor of love...will no doubt tear down walls, build bridges, and ultimately reveal the authentic heart of Christ to this and future generations. He or she who has an ear, let him hear!

~ Bishop Jim Swilley (Founder and Senior Pastor – Church In The Now)

CONTENTS

The Holy Bible of Inclusion

Part 1 - INTRODUCTION

-Letter from the Author-
-Invitation of Truth-
-Prayer of Surrender-

✳

-OUR GOALS-

✳

-THE BIBLE... its ORIGINS and PURPOSE-

✳

-INTRODUCTION-

✳

Who is going to harm you if you are eager to do good? But even if you should suffer for what is right, you are blessed. "Do not fear their threats; do not be frightened." But in your hearts revere Christ as Lord. ***ALWAYS BE PREPARED TO GIVE AN ANSWER TO EVERYONE WHO ASKS YOU TO GIVE A REASON FOR THE HOPE THAT YOU HAVE****. But do this with gentleness and respect, keeping a clear conscience, so that those who speak maliciously against your good behavior in Christ may be ashamed of their slander. For it is better, if it is God's will, to suffer for doing good than for doing evil. For Christ also suffered once for sins, the righteous for the unrighteous, to bring you to God.*
I Peter 3:13-18 NIV

Then He opened their minds so they could understand the Scriptures.
Luke 24:45 – NIV

Letter from the Author...

Dear Seeker and Student of God's Word,

I speak a blessing upon you for setting your heart and intention to study the Word of God as captured and expressed in the Judeo-Christian scriptures, tradition, culture and mindset. Although eternal truth cannot be completely contained in, nor confined to, any singular book, concept or even religion, the purpose of this book specifically is to deal with and reveal the truth that is found and often times concealed in the Holy Bible. This book is designed to voice and uncover hidden biblical truths to the Christian mind.

Allow me to say from the outset that I am at peace with me...and with you! My desire is not to try to prove my theology to be right and that of others to be wrong. If I have done so in the past, I have since learned that debate can be divisive, and the egoic need to be right can, in the end, unconsciously make you wrong. Furthermore, I cannot claim to be a "Oneness" teacher and be void of the realization that at the very heart of this idea is (and must be) tolerance and celebration for diversity of thought. After all, *the Body is made whole by what every part supplies.*

Each one of our individual journeys is both sacred and spiritual. We all progress at our own pace. And, we all evolve in our own space. To be open and honest, my spiritual journey has led me to as many questions as it has to answers. Like King David, my earnest desire is to *dwell in the presence of God and to INQUIRE of the Lord.* All I ask is that we honor one another on our particular searches for truth and acknowledge that *Truth is a Journey, not a Destination!* And as it relates to me personally, all I ask is that you recognize my love for God, for truth, for God's Word and for God's people. It is improbable, and perhaps even impossible, for us all to be on the exact same page theologically. However, it is possible to value the perspective of others, and it is healthy to allow *iron to sharpen iron.* I respect your journey and growth. I hope that whatever your truth is, and is becoming, that you see my truth is living and moving and having its being in me - and as me.

Let us be agreed that as we grow together in truth that we not confess our theology is changing – but rather that we recognize the fact that God is taking us from *glory to glory!* God has continuously revealed unchanging truth throughout the ages *line upon line, precept upon precept.* Eternal truth does not change over time but is revealed and embraced over time. Honestly, love is the only universal and timeless absolute that I have discovered thus far. So to all who will read this *HOLY BIBLE OF INCLUSION...* I say **"NAMASTE"** – that which is holy in me recognizes that which is holy in you. My earnest prayer is that this book will reveal Christ TO us, IN us, THROUGH us and AS us.

Pro-love,

D. E.

INVITATION OF TRUTH

As we journey through the Word of God together, searching for hidden truths that have remained concealed for many years, we must invite the Spirit of God to guide us into TRUTH. If you are in agreement, read aloud this simple Invitation of Truth:

My mind is alert and my Spirit is open to receive Truth. I acknowledge that Truth is not reserved only to what I already know and is not merely restricted to concepts with which I am already familiar. As beauty is in the eye of the beholder – Truth is in the ear, heart and mind of the perceiver.

PRAYER OF SURRENDER

This prayer acknowledges that we are completely surrendered and declares that the Holy Spirit has our permission to add to or subtract from our beliefs about the truths that we already possess. If you are in agreement, read aloud this simple Prayer of Surrender:

Spirit of Truth, CARRY me where You will; BRING to me what You will; TAKE from me what You will...I am surrendered. Amen.

OUR GOALS

1) To promote the idea that **GOD IS LOVE!**

> ➤ If our study in the scriptures leads us to a better understanding of God's love and to a more powerful expression of the love of God – this book will have accomplished its goal.

Dear friends, let us love one another, for love comes from God.
Everyone who loves has been born of God and knows God.
Whoever does not love does not know God, because God is love.
Whoever lives in love lives in God, and God in him.
I John 4:7-8, 16 - NIV

2) To **MAGNIFY GOD!**

> ➤ We will be equipped to effectively communicate to others that God is bigger than any idea of holding grudges, getting even or keeping a meticulous record of our sins.

> ➤ We will be prepared to show through our study of scripture that God is Creator, and is fully able to teach, discipline, purify, maintain and parent His Creation.

I will bless the LORD at all times; His praise shall continually
be in my mouth. My soul shall make its boast in the LORD; The
humble shall hear of it and be glad. Oh, MAGNIFY the LORD with
me, And let us exalt His name together.
Psalm 34:1-3 - NKJV

3) To reveal a **STRONG, VICTORIOUS JESUS!**

> ➤ We will be able to show a conquering Last Adam who is much more powerful and successful than the first Adam was…or ever could be.

> ➤ We will become knowledgeable of the FINISHED WORK of God's Grace through the atoning work of Jesus the Christ.

For if, when we were God's enemies, we were RECONCILED to him through the death of his Son, how much more, having BEEN RECONCILED, shall we be saved through his life! Not only is this so, but we also rejoice in God through our Lord Jesus Christ, through whom we have now RECEIVED RECONCILIATION. Consequently, just as the result of one trespass was condemnation for ALL MEN, so also the result of one act of righteousness was justification that brings life for ALL MEN.
Romans 5:10-11, 18 - NIV

Jesus knew that his mission was now finished, and to fulfill Scripture he said, "I am thirsty." A jar of sour wine was sitting there, so they soaked a sponge in it, put it on a hyssop branch, and held it up to his lips. When Jesus had tasted it, he said, "It is finished!" Then he bowed his head and released his spirit.
John 19:28-30 – New Living

4) To be **EMPOWERED as LEADERS** and **EQUIPPED as TEACHERS** for the **WORK OF OUR MINISTRY!**

> ➤ We will be ready to answer, TEACH and instruct others in the deep mysteries of the Love of God.

And He Himself gave some to be apostles, some prophets, some evangelists, and some pastors and teachers, for the equipping of the saints for the work of ministry, for the edifying of the body of Christ, till we all come to the unity of the faith and of the knowledge of the Son of God, to a perfect man, to the measure of the stature of the fullness of Christ; that we should no longer be children, tossed to and fro and carried about with every wind of doctrine, by the trickery of men, in the cunning craftiness of deceitful plotting, but, speaking the truth in love, may grow up in all things into Him who is the head - Christ - from whom the whole body, joined and knit together by what every joint supplies, according to the effective working by which every part does its share, causes growth of the body for the edifying of itself in love.
Ephesians 4:11-16 - NKJV

We are all LEADERS in some capacity and are being further prepared to LEAD. Consider these definitions of leadership as we accept the responsibility to LEAD others into truth.

Definitions of a Leader:
  ➤ One who leads and guides by means of influence or by way of power.
  ➤ One who can direct people toward the achievement of a goal.
  ➤ One who is not afraid to jeopardize himself, or those around him, to achieve a result that will be for the betterment of the corporate good.

As we embark on this journey toward deeper biblical understanding, I call to the leader that resides in you...you're going to need it.

THE BIBLE ... its ORIGINS and PURPOSE

1) The Bible is not a book. It is a collection of 66 books (from the Greek word *ta biblia*, which means "the scrolls" or "the books"), written by 40 different authors (including shepherds, fishermen, kings, farmers, scribes, poets, priests and prophets) in different languages over a period of 1,500 years to different people groups who spoke different languages, in different generations, and for different reasons.

2) The Bible is divinely Inspired but penned and communicated by humans (refer to "I Don't Know...the Way of Knowing" pgs. 122-125). We should honor the divine and human aspects of the Bible in the same way that we must revere Jesus as Son of God (divine) and as Son of Man (human). The Bible is both divine and human, Spirit and flesh, Supernatural and natural. The Bible is both God's Word to man and man's word about God. The Bible is not to be worshipped as *God*, but to be revered as a *guide*.

3) The Bible was written in Hebrew and Greek.

> ➢ Portions of the Bible were translated into English from 700-1350 AD.
> ➢ 1380-1397 John Wycliffe translated entire Bible into English (was forced to avoid many attempts on his life).
> ➢ 1526 William Tyndale produced first New Testament translation from the original Greek.
> ➢ 1536 Tyndale is burned at the stake for his translation work.

4) The Purpose of the Bible is to bring Revelation. The Bible is a guide leading us to a greater understanding of the nature of God and God's relationship to all of creation.

Going through a long line of prophets, God has been addressing our ancestors in different ways for centuries. Recently he spoke to

26

*us directly through his Son. By his Son, God created the world in
the beginning, and it will all belong to the Son at the end. This Son
perfectly mirrors God, and is stamped with God's nature. He holds
everything together by what he says—powerful words!*
Hebrews 1:1-3 – The Message Bible

5) The Spirit always supersedes the Letter. Jesus continually
challenged those of literal mindedness to see the truths contained in
scripture in a more metaphorical, figurative, parabolic and spiritual
way.

*He has made us competent as ministers of a new covenant—
not of the letter but of the Spirit; for the letter kills,
but the Spirit gives life.*
II Corinthians 3:6 - NIV

6) The Bible must be Rightly Divided - not Wrongly Connected!
Many doctrines of men resemble the monster Frankenstein; sewn
together to create fear and terror. Read every scripture with regard
to culture and context.

*Be diligent to present yourself approved to God, a worker who
does not need to be ashamed, rightly dividing the word of truth.*
II Timothy 2:15 - NKJV

7) The Bible contains many contradictions. Biblical contradiction
should be embraced and researched rather than denied, ignored
and kept hidden away in shame. These contradictions can serve to
give us different perspectives of how different men perceived God
in different ways and in different times. Each and every biblical
contradiction reveals a different aspect of God; reveals a different
perspective of God's relationship with man; reveals a different

glimpse of God's instruction to man. And, usually somewhere between the polarities of these contradictions lies eternal truth and a necessary balance and moderation. Different doesn't mean wrong or bad. It just means different.

Truth is held in tension.
-Ern Baxter

8) The CANON of scripture. Several books exist that were not included in the final Canon of scripture. This does not mean that these books are evil or satanic. Constantine, Emperor of Rome, was eager to unify the Roman Empire. He knew that as long as there remained religious contention and argument between the popular Christian bishops, the empire would not conquer the rest of the world. Unity among the people was vital. He gathered the bishops from the surrounding areas for a meeting – historically we refer to this gathering as *The Council of Nicea.* Their task was to meet and ultimately to emerge unified in thought and theology. It was at this council meeting that much of the early church father's ideas were lost to us.

9) There is No "Authorized" Version of the Bible. King James was the King of England who authorized men to translate the Bible into the Old English dialect. Try to remember that Jesus did not speak in Old English. Neither Jesus, nor Moses nor Elijah nor any of the prophets were English – they were Eastern.

10) The Bible is GOOD NEWS. If we consider three landmark events in the Bible (the Creation account, the birth of Jesus of Nazareth and the Last words of John the Revelator) we will find a common thread connecting God's plan for humanity.

➤ God was acting **REDEMPTIVELY** in creation!

In the beginning God created the heavens and the earth.
Genesis 1:1 KJV

-The word *created* is *bara* in the Hebrew – translated as "to reshape or carve out." Even in Moses' telling of his understanding of the account of Creation – we see God acting redemptively to reshape what had become chaotic.

➤ The entrance of Jesus brings Good News / **REDEMPTION!**
It is recorded that at the birth of Jesus, the angels declared –

"Glory to God in the highest, And on earth peace,
goodwill toward men!"
Luke 2:14 – KJV

Theology that will stand the test of time will accomplish three things: it will bring *Glory to God*; it will create *Peace on Earth*; and it will proclaim God's *Goodwill toward all men* and *foster Goodwill between all men.*

➤ God is **REDEMPTIVE** and restorative as we come to the close of the Bible. When we read the last words of John the revelator we find a *new heaven and new earth*; God is now *dwelling with men*; and *ALL THINGS are made new (Revelation 21:1, 3, 5)*!

INTRODUCTION

I could say "the glass is half full" and then say of the same glass that it is also "half empty" – and each of these opposing statements would be strangely true, correct, accurate. It is true. The same glass that is half full is also half empty. Both of these statements are "right." Whether we see the glass half full or half empty does not reveal accuracy or correctness or rightness about the water or the glass. How we view the glass only brings to light our personal perspective and level of consciousness.

In many Christian circles, there has been much theological debate around the doctrine of *Universal Salvation*. Other "less threatening" offshoot names associated with Universal Salvation are: *Ultimate Reconciliation*, the *Finished Work of Grace* and the *Restoration of All Things*. However, *INCLUSION* is the name (at least for the past decade) that has received the greater majority of attention. From an exhaustive, thorough study of the scriptures (including both Old and New Testaments) – we can, and will, accurately prove that Universal Salvation is an original, sound and recurring doctrine throughout the whole Bible. Yet, we also find a consistent biblical pattern that would line up with a more fundamentalist or evangelical expression and interpretation.

So, how do we choose?

Which Bible do we read?

The Universal, Progressive, *Inclusive* Bible?

The Fundamentalist, Evangelical, *Exclusive* Bible?

The Bible is a holy book (or a collection of 66 holy books) containing contrasting (even contradicting) truths. And, it is designed that way. The contradictions are there intentionally to encourage growth and a greater depth of understanding. They are meant to catapult us into higher revelations. The Bible is a progression of man's process of wrestling with the unending truth of an eternal God. The Bible is a beautiful story of humanity's struggle and surrender to becoming divine. And, along this journey we utilize the Bible, not to declare or prove specific doctrines as absolute truth – but, we corporately use the Bible as a mirror to show us where we are individually on the path to enlightenment. If the Bible contains purposeful contradicting truths...then the Bible we choose to read (whether inclusive or exclusive) only reveals our personal level of spiritual growth and our degree of awakened consciousness.

In the final analysis, this "argument" has proven to be counterproductive to achieving a cohesive collaboration and a closer common union in the greater Body of Christ. As long as the ultimate goal, from either viewpoint, is to prove someone or something to be right or wrong (the glass to be half full or half empty) we will never see the beauty and necessity of celebrating a diversity of expression and function in the same Body.

Inevitably, when theological arguments ensue, people become polarized to one position or the other, allowing very little room for open-minded discussion, thus effectively preventing any possibility of learning anything from someone who may have a perspective other than their own. As a fourth generation preacher, I have seen my share of doctrinal schism, and have heard of even more. Biblical argument is just about as old as the Bible itself. And, Christianity is an extremely scripture-driven religion. Someone who has been raised with the Bible as if it were a long-standing trusted family member will usually not even give consideration to an unfamiliar spiritual concept without first being shown some sort of foundational scriptural reference or evidence. If I had a dime for every time I have heard someone say – "Show it to me in the Word" – I would... well, have a lot of dimes.

On an even larger scale than merely within the sphere of Christianity, arguments that eventually escalate into wars are fought all over the world between people who think their holy book is the true "WORD of God" and that all other holy books are wrong. Many are willing to die for this cause and have done so, and will continue to do so until we realize that the Word of God cannot be contained in any one book. All holy books exist to guide us to the Spirit of God – not to be worshipped. The Bible is not God. It was written by men, to men, and is largely about man's search for God. Perhaps the writers were divinely inspired men, but still…men. The Bible contains God, but it also contains humanity.

This book is designed to give extensive, even exhaustive, specific scriptural references and evidence for the ancient doctrine of Universal Salvation. In other words, this book will *Show it to you in the Word!*

This book will provide a solid biblical foundation for the ideas of an Inclusive Gospel. It will not, however, attempt to prove someone or something right, or even wrong. From the same Bible one can scripturally prove, and then disprove, many different theological precepts and positions. From the same Christian canon we can prove and then disprove, or at least dispute, Universal Salvation. If proving and disproving the same theological position from the same Bible is possible, then we must accept that this is not about *biblical accuracy*. This is more specifically about revealing our personal perspective and uncovering the corporate level of consciousness in the Body of Christ.

The Bible is full of opposing or contradicting thoughts and views on several issues (and many times the same author is seemingly on both sides of a theological view…both *for* and then *against* the exact same issue). These examples only provide us with further reason for understanding that the argument of Universal Salvation is not about biblical accuracy – but about revealing consciousness. Consider just a few of these biblical contradictions:

➤ **David teaches both our innate sinfulness – and our innate god-like divinity:**

Surely I was sinful at birth, sinful from the time my
mother conceived me.
Psalm 51:5 - NIV

I praise you because I am fearfully and wonderfully made; your
works are wonderful, I know that full well.
Psalm 139:14 - NIV

➤ **Paul writes to promote and denounce slavery:**

There is neither Jew nor Greek, there is neither slave nor free,
there is neither male nor female; for you are all one in
Christ Jesus.
Galatians 3:28 - NKJV

Slaves, obey your earthly masters in everything; and do it, not only
when their eye is on you and to win their favor, but with sincerity
of heart and reverence for the Lord.
Colossians 3:22 (and Ephesians 6:5) - NIV

➤ **Jesus discourages and also encourages the use of the sword:**

And suddenly, one of those who were with Jesus stretched out his
hand and drew his sword, struck the servant of the high priest, and
cut off his ear. But Jesus said to him, "Put your sword in its place,

for all who take the sword will perish by the sword. Or do you think that I cannot now pray to My Father, and He will provide Me with more than twelve legions of angels?"
Matthew 26:51-53 NKJV

Then He said to them, "But now, he who has a money bag, let him take it, and likewise a knapsack; and he who has no sword, let him sell his garment and buy one."
Luke 22:36 - NKJV

➢ **Peter teaches that a wife can win an unbelieving husband by her conduct. While Paul basically tells the wife of an unbelieving husband to let him leave:**

Wives, likewise, be submissive to your own husbands, that even if some do not obey the word, they, without a word, may be won by the conduct of their wives, when they observe your chaste conduct accompanied by fear.
I Peter 3:1-2 - NKJV

But if the unbeliever leaves, let him do so. A believing man or woman is not bound in such circumstances; God has called us to live in peace. How do you know, wife, whether you will save your husband? Or, how do you know, husband, whether you will save your wife?
I Corinthians 7:15-16 - NKJV

➢ **Paul teaches the necessity of faith for salvation...and also boldly proclaims that God does not depend upon man's faith:**

*That if you confess with your mouth, "Jesus is Lord," and believe
in your heart that God raised him from the dead, you will be saved.
For it is with your heart that you believe and are justified, and it is
with your mouth that you confess and are saved.*
Romans 10:9-10 - NIV

*What if some did not have faith? Will their lack of faith nullify
God's faithfulness? Not at all! Let God be true,
and every man a liar.*
Romans 3:3-4 - NIV

These seeming contradictions should not serve as ammunition to
destroy the Bible, nor should they serve as impetus to throw out
the Bible altogether. Better that they should reveal to us that truth
comes to us all in a progression! And, we must be willing to make
the journey with the Spirit of God – a daily journey being built *line
upon line; precept upon precept; here a little; there a little.* An
unchanging God is not changing! God is simply taking us *from
glory to glory.* We are engaged in a lifetime (or many lifetimes) of
receiving more and more revelation from God.

Allow me to give you a glimpse at perhaps the greatest progression
ever achieved by humanity (only a glimpse because we will go into
extensive scriptural research on this matter in a later section entitled
– *Jesus, and the Christ*). What progression is this? The progression
of Jesus of Nazareth…becoming the Christ – the progression of
Jesus, the Savior of the Jews…becoming the Christ, Savior of the
World!

In this passage from Matthew we find that Jesus sees Himself as
Savior – but only the Savior of the "Lost sheep of Israel." Jesus even
refers to this Canaanite woman, and to her people, as *dogs* (not even
worthy of the truths that the Jewish people knew and understood)!

However, when the woman responded in faith – she jolted Jesus out of His culturalistic, tribalistic, exclusive, limited mindset. In other words, she awakened the Universal Christ within Jesus of Nazareth. Jesus began as Savior of the lost sheep of Israel – but He progressed into becoming the Savior of the World! The truth is that Jesus was the Christ, Savior of the World from the beginning – but Jesus (the man) had come to this realization about Himself by way of a progression of revelation.

Leaving that place, Jesus withdrew to the region of Tyre and Sidon. A Canaanite woman from that vicinity came to him, crying out, "Lord, Son of David, have mercy on me! My daughter is suffering terribly from demon-possession." Jesus did not answer a word. So his disciples came to him and urged him, "Send her away, for she keeps crying out after us." He answered, "I WAS SENT ONLY TO THE LOST SHEEP OF ISRAEL." The woman came and knelt before him. "Lord, help me!" she said. He replied, "It is not right to take the children's bread and toss it to their dogs." "Yes, Lord," she said, "but even the dogs eat the crumbs that fall from their masters' table. "Then Jesus answered, "Woman, you have great faith! Your request is granted." And her daughter was healed from that very hour.
Matthew 15:21-28 - NIV

In the 4ᵗʰ Chapter of John we see that Jesus has now broadened His perspective and His desire to reach those outside of his culture and religion. He has widened the scope of His earthly ministry from exclusively being to the lost sheep of Israel – to understanding that His ministry was to the whole world! Notice that Jesus now understands why he had to go through Samaria – a place that Jews almost never frequented (as Jews and Samaritans had no dealings with each other).

Therefore, when the Lord knew that the Pharisees had heard that Jesus made and baptized more disciples than John (though Jesus Himself did not baptize, but His disciples), He left Judea and departed again to Galilee. BUT HE NEEDED TO GO THROUGH SAMARIA.
John 4:1-4 - NKJV

And many of the Samaritans of that city believed in Him because of the word of the woman who testified, "He told me all that I ever did." So when the Samaritans had come to Him, they urged Him to stay with them; and He stayed there two days. And many more believed because of His own word. Then they said to the woman, "Now we believe, not because of what you said, for we ourselves have heard Him and we know that this is indeed THE CHRIST, THE SAVIOR OF THE WORLD."
John 4:39-42 - NKJV

…From Jesus, the Savior of the lost sheep of Israel…to the Christ, the Savior of the World. If Jesus *grew in grace and in truth* – we also will and must follow His example!

However, as long as we insist on eating from the Tree of the Knowledge of Good and Evil we will always find ourselves outside of God's original intention and environment for mankind. How do we get back to God's original intention for man? We must go back and do what we were told to do in the Garden. We must eat only from the Tree of Life. What is the difference between these two trees? From the Tree of the Knowledge of Good and Evil we get labels, denominations, separation, arguments, judgment. It represents this physical world with all its opposites: good and evil; light and darkness. The Tree of Life, on the other hand, represents the spiritual realm where duality does not exist. Here we find only the way of love and mercy and the interconnectedness of all forms of God's creation.

So, the objective of this book is not to prove or disprove concepts that can be substantiated as both true and untrue from the same Bible. The ideas set forth here are designed to reveal to you your level of consciousness, and to promote a lifetime blessed by a progressive flow of revelation from the Spirit of God. The motivation behind this book is to show the need for inclusivity of the manifold expressions in the same Body. Yes, the message and method may vary from church to church. However, the mission and mandate remains the same: *to reconnect humanity to God by revealing Christ.*

Apostles and Early Church Fathers, Paul and Peter provide an excellent example of this as they worshiped the same God and served the same Christ. Very few, if any, would disagree on this. Their mission and mandate were the same: *to reconnect humanity to God by revealing Christ.* Yet, the methods they utilized, and even the messages they preached, tended to be quite different. So different, in fact, that it spawned a conflict that led to confrontation (Paul writing about this confrontation with Peter even uses the words - *I withstood Peter to his face*). Then one day, Paul begins to receive a revelation from God:

There are different kinds of gifts, but the same Spirit. There are different kinds of service, but the same Lord. There are different kinds of working, but the same God works all of them in all men. Now to each one the manifestation of the Spirit is given for the common good. The body is a unit, though it is made up of many parts; and though all its parts are many, they form one body. So it is with Christ... Now the body is not made up of one part but of many. If the foot should say, "Because I am not a hand, I do not belong to the body," it would not for that reason cease to be part of the body. And if the ear should say, "Because I am not an eye, I do not belong to the body," it would not for that reason cease to be part of the body. If the whole body were an eye, where would the sense of hearing be? If the whole body were an ear, where would the sense of smell be? But in fact God has arranged the parts in the

body, every one of them, just as he wanted them to be. If they were all one part, where would the body be? As it is, there are many parts, but one body. The eye cannot say to the hand, "I don't need you!" And the head cannot say to the feet, "I don't need you!"... Now you are the body of Christ, and each one of you is a part of it.
I Corinthians 12:4-7, 12, 14-21, 27 (New International Version)

Paul begins to understand and ultimately accept the truth that the Body of Christ is made up of distinct groups of people, who even though they may differ in expression, are all necessary for the Body to function properly. As part of this new revelation, Paul not only entertains, but actively encourages the thought that different parts of the Body should maintain their unique expressions for the overall health and growth of the Body. Simultaneously, he beseeches the individual members to recognize, to affirm and to honor all of the other members of the Body – even though their functions often seem in opposition to one another. Finally, Paul personally applies this revelation to his attitude toward, and relationship with, Peter.

Instead, they saw that God had given me the responsibility of preaching the gospel to the Gentiles, just as he had given Peter the responsibility of preaching to the Jews. For the SAME GOD who worked through Peter as the apostle to the Jews also worked through me as the apostle to the Gentiles.
Galatians 2:7-8 (New Living Translation)

In other words, Paul realizes that Peter's ministry, mission and message, although very different, are just as valid and necessary as his own. It is worth noting that at no time in Paul's process of developing tolerance for Peter and his expression in the Body does Paul accuse Peter of not being a part of the Body of Christ due to the fact that Peter's specific function is different from his. Paul and Peter preached and presented notably dissimilar views of the same

God. They kept company with extremely divergent people groups (at least publicly). I would venture to guess that if they were still alive today they might find themselves on opposite sides of theological arguments; on opposing teams over social issues; even in separate political parties with polarized cultural opinions. However, despite their vast disparities and their utter uniqueness, Paul and Peter never attempted to excommunicate one another from the Body of Christ.

This book is written to show the vast diversity that exists in the Body of Christ and to provide an abundance of scriptural reference and exhaustive evidence that the ancient concepts of Universal Salvation, Ultimate Reconciliation, The Restoration of All Things – or "Inclusion" – are just as much a viable part of the Christian Scriptures and Christian Church as is the mindset that would oppose these ideals. The goal then is to encourage a broader understanding and a greater tolerance for the many doctrines that all have the right to exist under the same umbrella of Christianity. The goal is to re-member the Body of Christ. The goal is to truly become One!

The Holy Bible of Inclusion

Part II – UNIVERSAL SALVATION
(Ultimate Reconciliation, The Restoration of All Things, "Inclusion")

——◆——

-Concentrated Statement about Universal Salvation-
*

-Universal Salvation-
*

-Early Universalist Church Fathers-
*

-Modern Church Fathers on Universal Salvation-
*

-Adam versus Jesus-
*

-Reconciling the Mind (not the Soul) of Man-
*

-The Eternal Christ-
*

-All is Christ's-
*

-Faith IN Faith?-
*

-The WILL of GOD? Or the WILL of Man?-
✱

-Atonement Made for ALL-
✱

-Be Cautious of the Elder Brother Syndrome-
✱

-The ALLNESS of God in the Old Testament-
✱

-Review-
✱

CONCENTRATED STATEMENT ON UNIVERSAL SALVATION

The pattern, promotion, preaching and practice of magnifying a *Finished Work of Adam* over the perverse idea of an *Unfinished Work of Christ*, must be retracted, rethought, and re-presented. In this section we will gain, or better REGAIN, a proper perspective of the limited power of the first Adam, and of the limitless providence of the Second Adam. In short, the GOOD NEWS is that the bad news was wrong – *"if ALL MEN died in Adam...ALL MEN live in Christ" (Romans 5; 1 Corinthians 15).*

UNIVERSAL SALVATION

Universal Salvation, Universal Reconciliation, or sometimes simply Universalism, is commonly defined and held as the belief that all people have received salvation, or will at some point receive salvation, because of the love, mercy and providential will of God. Several different streams of thought exist as part of the vast river of Universalism. Some in the river of Universalism believe that all souls have already been reconciled to God and have been imputed salvation as a result of the *finished work* of Jesus at Calvary whether they are conscious of their reconciliation or not.

Some believe that many are still *working out their salvation with fear and trembling* – and that even though the whole world will be saved, there is a necessary purging as part of the salvation process. Still others believe that confession of and a belief in Jesus as personal savior are necessary, and that *every knee will (someday) bow and every tongue will (eventually) confess Jesus as Lord.* In reference to the diversity of Universalist ideas regarding the way in which God will reconcile humanity, we might say it this way: "We *WERE* saved, We *ARE* saved and We *ARE BEING* saved!" Although there are several branches of Universalism, one central theme remains the same – God will reclaim all of His "stuff" and not one soul will be lost eternally.

As we begin to search the scriptures for a foundation and for evidence of a pervasive current of Universal Salvation, let us be reminded of one of the initial goals for this book (#3- To reveal a STRONG, VICTORIOUS JESUS! We will be able to show a conquering Last Adam who is much more powerful and successful than the first Adam was…or ever could be). Furthermore, if we believe that John the revelator prophetically saw that the *kingdoms of this world have become the Kingdoms of our God and of His Christ (Revelation 11:15)* then it should not be a stretch for the mind to perceive or foreign for the ear to hear that ALL SOULS belong to God! If the kingdoms of this world will or *have been* reclaimed by God, then the souls of this world *have been* reclaimed by God as well. In other words, why would God care more about kingdoms than souls? The kingdoms of the world AND the souls of the world belong to God!

The earth is the LORD's, and everything in it, the world,
and ALL WHO LIVE IN IT.
Psalm 24:1 – NIV (also I Corinthians 10:26, 28)

A mindset that will keep us from truth, or rather from a constant flow of truth, is one that perceives it already knows all truth. Strangely enough, the hyper-religious mind hesitates to wade into the ever-flowing river of God's proceeding truth because it assumes that it already has all truth. Notice here in the next verse that Jesus declares to the religious mind and mindset of His day that it would be preferable for them to be blind, or completely ignorant of spiritual truths than to perceive they know it all. But because they indeed had this mindset, they struggled to receive the words and truth Jesus came to impart.

Some of the Pharisees said, "This man is not from God, for he does not keep the Sabbath." But others asked, "How can a sinner do such miraculous signs?" So they were divided Jesus said, "For judgment I have come into this world, so that the blind will see and THOSE WHO SEE WILL BECOME BLIND." Some Pharisees who were with him heard him say this and asked, "What? Are we blind too?" Jesus said, "If you were blind, you would not be guilty of sin; but now that YOU CLAIM YOU CAN SEE, your guilt remains.
John 9: 16, 39-41 - NIV

It was the spiritually blind of Jesus' day who were able to see and hear the truth Jesus came to bring to humanity. As we examine the scriptures on the subject of Universal Salvation, I hope you will attempt to keep an open and neutral mind. If you can't go as far as to rid your mind entirely of its preconditioning and preconception, perhaps you can temporarily suspend what you already know of God, in order that you might know more of God.

"I have become eager to suspend what I thought I knew about God in order to know Him in a way I didn't know was possible."
Bishop Carlton Pearson – ("The Gospel of Inclusion")

Many critics of Universal Salvation claim that it is a new doctrine, a false doctrine and a doctrine reflective of the *Last Days* that will attract those who will not *endure sound doctrine.*

For the time will come when men will not put up with sound doctrine. Instead, to suit their own desires, they will gather around them a great number of teachers to say what their itching ears want to hear. They will turn their ears away from the truth and turn aside to myths.
II Timothy 4:3-4 NIV

EARLY UNIVERSALIST CHURCH FATHERS

After we research this doctrine we will discover several things. We will find that Universal Salvation is not some newfangled anti-Christ doctrine of devils. We will discover that Universal Salvation is an ancient doctrine – as ancient as the Christian church and nearly as old as the Bible itself. Before Constantine silenced the voices of these Early Church Fathers via the Council of Nicea, there existed a predominant understanding and celebration of the *Finished Work of Christ*. Actually, two of the three original Christian Theological Universities were *Universalist* in their theological foundation and doctrinal expression. Yet, in order to unify the Roman Empire under one prevailing theological position, Constantine squashed any theological differences that existed between the early church bishops, leaders and teachers.

Thankfully we have just a few fragments from the writings of these divinely inspired men of God who perceived the awesomeness of God and taught a doctrine that both magnifies the work of Jesus the Christ and gives us evidence that Universal Salvation is anything but a new doctrine.

Stronger than all the evils in the soul is the WORD, and the healing power that dwells in Him, and this healing He applies, according to the will of God, TO EVERYMAN. The consummation of all things is the destruction of evil...to quote Zephaniah: "My determination to gather the nations, that I am assembling the kings, to pour upon them Mine indignation, even say all my fierce anger, for all the earth shall be devoured with the FIRE OF MY JEALOUSY. For then will I turn to the people a pure language that they may ALL call upon the name of the Lord, to serve Him with ONE CONSENT"... Consider carefully the promise, that ALL SHALL CALL UPON THE NAME OF THE LORD, AND SERVE HIM WITH ONE CONSENT.
Origen – (185-254 A.D.)

Through Origen's writings we are introduced to a recurring concept among many Early Church Fathers who were Universalist in their understanding of salvation. The concept: Jesus can and will save ALL MEN...BY ANY MEANS NECESSARY! Some will be saved by their own surrender, and others will be saved by the *all consuming-purging fire of the Holy Spirit.*

In the end and consummation of the Universe ALL ARE TO BE RESTORED INTO THEIR ORIGINAL HARMONIOUS STATE, and we ALL shall be made ONE BODY and be united once more into a perfect man and the prayer of our Savior shall be fulfilled that ALL MAY BE ONE.
St. Jerome – (331-420 A.D.)

For it is evident that God will in truth be all in all when there shall be no evil in existence, when EVERY CREATED BEING is at harmony with itself and EVERY TONGUE shall confess that Jesus Christ is Lord: when EVERY CREATURE shall have BEEN MADE ONE BODY.
Gregory of Nyssa – (335-390 A.D.)

We can set NO LIMITS to the agency of the Redeemer: to redeem, to rescue, to discipline, in His work, and so will He continue to operate AFTER THIS LIFE. ALL MEN ARE HIS...for either the Lord does not care for ALL MEN...or He does care for ALL. For He is Savior; not of some and of others not...and HOW IS HE SAVIOR AND LORD, IF NOT THE SAVIOR AND LORD OF ALL? For ALL THINGS are arranged with a view to the SALVATION OF THE UNIVERSE by the Lord of the universe both generally and particularly.
Clement of Alexandria

Observe here Clement of Alexandria's balanced view of Salvation. He magnifies Christ by declaring that there can exist no restriction on the Savior's power and ability to save. He makes the strong claim that Jesus is Savior of ALL MEN and Lord of ALL MEN – and then adds if He is not Savior OF ALL...He is not Savior AT ALL! Yet, Clement also points out that a necessary part of the salvation of all men may include the disciplining of some men *after this life* (or a temporary purging in hell that brings about salvation – we'll get to that later).

MODERN CHURCH FATHERS on UNIVERSAL SALVATION

But in one thing, I would go beyond strict orthodoxy - I am a convinced Universalist. I believe that in the end all men will be gathered into the love of God.
William Barclay – (A Spiritual Autobiography)

Very few unsaved people today have ever really heard the "Good News." Why? Because too many Christians are busy telling the world God is mad at them, and telling them that they're terrible and wrong. Some call that "good news" but it's not, and it's not what God has commissioned us to share. He's given us the "word of reconciliation!" He's sent us to tell the news that God has restored harmony and fellowship between Himself and men. ALL MEN. NOT JUST BELIEVERS. Not just the people in your church, BUT EVERYONE! That's right. The worst old reprobate sinner in the world is every bit reconciled to God as you are. Look at Romans 5:10 and you'll see what I mean. It says "when we were enemies, we were reconciled to God by the death of his son." Reconciled. That word is past tense. God has ALREADY RESTORED FELLOWSHIP between Himself and THE WORLD. He did it when there was NOT ONE PERSON, except Jesus, who BELIEVED in the NEW BIRTH. He did it when the entire world was lying in sin. Through the death and resurrection of Jesus, God has cleansed and forgiven and restored to Himself EVERY MAN, WOMAN and CHILD on the face of the earth. All any of us have to do now is to receive it. That's the good word God has given us. That's the word we need to share with those who are lost. If we'll do it, I can almost guarantee you, they won't stay lost very long.
Kenneth Copeland – (Faith to Faith)

Notice that Pastor Kenneth Copeland declares time and again that the world is already reconciled to God whether they know it or not or believe it or not! Yet, he brings an important balance that a person can be reconciled to God and still be lost or unaware of their reconciliation and re-connectedness to God. *Receiving Reconciliation* is therefore not an attempt to FINISH a work that has already been completed – but rather an ACKNOWLEDGMENT of the Finished Work of Christ.

Did you ever stop and think about it; salvation belongs to the sinner. Jesus already has bought the salvation of the worst sinner, just as he did for us. That's the reason he told us to go tell the sinner the Good News; go tell sinners they HAVE BEEN RECONCILED to God. But we never really told them that. We've told them God's mad at them and that He's counting up everything they've done wrong. Yet, the Bible says God isn't holding anything against the sinner! God says he's cancelled it out.
Kenneth E. Hagin, Sr. – (The Authority of the Believer)

I think everybody that loves Christ, or knows Christ, WHETHER THEY'RE CONSCIOUS OF IT OR NOT, they're members of the Body of Christ. And, that's what God is doing today; He's calling people out of the world for His name. Whether they come from the Muslim world, or the Buddhist world, or the Christian world, or the NON-BELIEVING world, they are members of the Body of Christ because they've been called by God. THEY MAY NOT EVEN KNOW THE NAME OF JESUS, but they know in their heart that they need something, and they turn to the only light that they have. AND, I THINK THEY'RE SAVED, AND THEY'RE GOING TO BE WITH US IN HEAVEN.
Billy Graham - (Television interview with Robert Schueller)

The entire world is saved; they just don't know it.
Carlton Pearson – (The Gospel of Inclusion)

Interestingly enough, this phrase *(The entire world is saved; they just don't know it)* is most often associated with Bishop Carlton Pearson – but was actually coined by Dr. T. L. Osborn on a live Christian broadcast while being interviewed by Bishop Pearson. Dr. T. L. Osborn has preached to more people face to face than any person in human history.

This is just a very brief list of noteworthy Modern Church Fathers who believe in and have given voice to the truth of Universal Salvation / Ultimate Reconciliation. It is no exaggeration to speculate that the Reverend Billy Graham and Dr. T. L. Osborn together have preached face to face (not on television) to hundreds of millions of people – if not billions.

It is also important to note that these men began their ministries with a very different perspective of scripture and salvation than they have come to know and preach in their later years. Reverend Billy Graham is historically known for his invitations to *sinners* to receive salvation. These calls for salvation have persuaded millions in stadiums across the globe to come to the altar. And very often, the invitation given was even laced with fear, and with the question – *If you were to die tonight, where would you spend eternity? In heaven? Or in hell?* Yet, as he progressed in truth, Reverend Graham began to understand more of the beautiful picture of God's complete and total reconciliation of mankind. In other words, Reverend Graham grew into the knowledge of the Good News of the Gospel. And, what is the Good News of the Gospel? The Good News is that the bad news was wrong – or at least incomplete.

As we will research later, both Paul and Jesus had a similar progression of truth as they matured in their ministries and in their awareness. These ancient and modern day examples of how truth progresses and grows within us give us a greater understanding of why truth must be celebrated as a journey, not as a destination. As we begin this unending journey toward greater truth and ever expanding revelation we must remember that *Faith comes by hearING*, not by having heard. Jesus said, *you have heard of old, but I say to you.* He also said, *Man shall not live by bread alone, but by every word that proceeds from the mouth of God.*

There is a constant flow of truth coming from God to us. And as we choose to flow and grow with God, our truth will inevitably continue to progress! The problem (or opportunity) we encounter is that when truth is placed in prison it will eventually break out. Many times as spiritual truth is setting itself free from human boundaries, the people who are housing this evolution of truth outgrow the confines of the Christian church because the traditional church is not known for defining truth as mysterious and unknowable. Actually, truth will inevitably outgrow any religion, as truth is bigger than anything manmade.

ADAM versus JESUS

Ultimate Reconciliation, Universal Salvation, the Restoration of All Things, and Inclusion receive constant criticism from those who perceive that these ancient truths somehow prostitute and diminish the blood of Jesus or minimize the work of Jesus on Calvary's Cross.

Referring again to *II Timothy 4:3-4* (*They will turn their ears away from the truth and turn aside to myths*) we must uncover one of the greatest theological myths that has ever been sold to, and bought by, Christianity. The myth to which I am referring is simply this: *Adam's work of disobedience* is more complete and more powerful than *Christ's work of obedience*.

The Church's actions and preaching, especially over the past few centuries, would lead an outside observer to believe this is the truth. On the contrary, however, the central idea of this message is that Jesus TRIUMPHS over sin, over any devil, over death, over any hell…and more specifically Jesus TRIUMPHS over Adam! Those who criticize this message for minimizing Jesus are unconsciously and blindly guilty of their own accusation. In truth, this message of Ultimate Reconciliation only declares that Jesus is AS POWERFUL as Adam – not more powerful. Yes, unbelievably, after we research the scriptures regarding Universal Salvation we will be faced with the reality that many in the Christian world have cried *heresy* and *false teaching* about a doctrine that merely says Jesus is AS POWERFUL as Adam! If equating Jesus to Adam stirs this much controversy, what will magnifying Jesus as greater than Adam cause? As we accept the idea that the Finished Work of Jesus is at least EQUAL to the finished work of Adam, then perhaps we may be able to someday sufficiently and soundly magnify Jesus ABOVE Adam!

For if, when we were God's enemies, we were RECONCILED to him through the death of his Son, how much more, having BEEN RECONCILED, shall we be saved through his life! Not only is this so, but we also rejoice in God through our Lord Jesus Christ, through whom we have now RECEIVED RECONCILIATION. Nevertheless, death reigned from the time of Adam to the time of Moses, even over those who did not sin by breaking a command, as did Adam, who was a pattern of the one to come. Consequently, just as the result of one trespass was condemnation for ALL MEN, so also the result of one act of righteousness was justification that brings life for ALL MEN.
Romans 5:10-11, 14, 18 - NIV

Even those who didn't sin precisely as Adam did by disobeying a specific command of God still had to experience this termination of life, this separation from God. But Adam, who got us into this, also points ahead to the One who will get us out of it.
Romans 5:14 - The Message Bible

Here it is in a nutshell: Just as one person did it wrong and got us in all this trouble with sin and death, another person did it right and got us out of it. But more than just getting us out of trouble, he got us into life!
Romans 5:18 – The Message Bible

All that passing laws against sin did was produce more lawbreakers. But sin didn't, and doesn't, have a chance in competition with the aggressive forgiveness we call grace. When it's sin versus grace, grace wins hands down. All sin can do is threaten us with death, and that's the end of it. Grace, because God is putting everything together again through the Messiah, invites us into life—a life that goes on and on and on, world without end.
Romans 5:20-21 The Message Bible

The fifth chapter of Romans is so powerful that I wanted to show it you in more than one translation. Although, no matter what translation you read, from King James to the New Living, every translation of the fifth chapter of Romans clearly reveals the Finished Work of Christ. Allow me to point out the Universalist nature of *Romans 5:*

-ALL MEN are *reconciled* to God through Christ (whether enemies or friends – whether conscious or unconscious of their reconciliation).

-Death was *imputed* to ALL MEN via Adam's disobedience (death was even imputed to those who had not sinned!)

-Just as Adam *imputed* death to ALL MEN (without their belief, choice, confession or consent) LIFE was *imputed* to ALL MEN through Christ (without their belief, choice, confession or consent).

For since death came through a man, the resurrection of the dead comes also through a man. For as IN ADAM ALL DIE, so IN CHRIST ALL WILL BE MADE ALIVE. So it is written: "The first man Adam became a living being"; the last Adam, a life-giving spirit. The spiritual did not come first, but the natural, and after that the spiritual. The first man was of the dust of the earth, the second man from heaven. As was the earthly man, so are those who are of the earth; and as is the man from heaven, so also are those who are of heaven. AND JUST AS WE HAVE BORNE THE LIKENESS OF THE EARTHLY MAN, SO SHALL WE BEAR THE LIKENESS OF THE MAN FROM HEAVEN.
I Corinthians 15:21-22, 45-49 - NIV

Notice again, the strong declaration that ALL DIE in Adam…and ALL will BE MADE ALIVE in Christ. This passage in Corinthians also takes us a bit further and shows us that we are not merely alive and reconciled to God because of Christ – we are also given the promise that even though we have reflected the likeness of Adam, we will certainly reflect the likeness of Christ.

RECONCILING THE MIND (not the SOUL) OF MAN

All this is from God, who reconciled us to himself through Christ and gave us the ministry of reconciliation: that God was reconciling the world to himself in Christ, not counting men's sins against them. And he has committed to us the message of reconciliation. We are therefore Christ's ambassadors, as though God were making his appeal through us. We implore you on Christ's behalf: Be reconciled to God.
II Corinthians 5:18-20 - NIV

Let us not steer away from an obvious and necessary question that this verse raises around the idea of Ultimate Reconciliation. Here is the question: If the world has BEEN RECONCILED to God, why does this passage say *"We implore you on Christ's behalf: Be reconciled to God?"* Here is the simple answer: The SOUL of man has been reconciled to God through Christ. Now we must reconcile the MIND of man to God by the preaching of the *Good News* – the Message of Reconciliation.

Allow me for a moment to be a bit philosophical. The work of Reconciliation did not originally happen in TIME... but in ETERNITY. The thirteenth chapter of the book of Revelation reveals to us that Jesus, the Lamb of God, was *slain from the foundation of the world.* In other words, Jesus went to Calvary in Eternity before he walked it out in Time. Even though we HAVE BEEN RECONCILED to God – we must now Reconcile our MINDS with what God has done...and did from the beginning. This next verse we will study in Colossians clearly reveals to us that the mind must be reconciled *(And you, who once were alienated and ENEMIES IN YOUR MIND)* in order to even be aware that the soul is reconciled.

*He is the image of the invisible God, the firstborn over all creation.
For by Him ALL THINGS were created that are in heaven and that
are on earth, visible and invisible, whether thrones or dominions or
principalities or powers. ALL THINGS were created THROUGH
HIM and FOR HIM. And He is before all things, and IN HIM ALL
THINGS CONSIST. And He is the head of the body, the church,
who is the beginning, the firstborn from the dead,
that in ALL THINGS He may have the preeminence.
For it pleased the Father that in Him all the fullness should dwell,
and by Him to RECONCILE ALL THINGS TO HIMSELF, by Him,
whether things on earth or things in heaven, having made peace
through the blood of His cross.
And you, who once were alienated and ENEMIES IN YOUR
MIND by wicked works, yet now He has reconciled in the body of
His flesh through death, to present you holy, and blameless,
and above reproach in His sight."*
Colossians 1:15-22 NIV

This passage from Colossians says that *ALL THINGS* are reconciled
to God through Christ (not just souls…all of creation). Yet, even
though the reconciliation between God and man is complete and
finished, the MIND of man must now PERCEIVE this reunion,
reconnection and reclamation of the SOUL.

*We are not like Moses, who would put a veil over his face to keep
the Israelites from gazing at it while the radiance was fading
away. But their MINDS WERE MADE DULL, for to this day the
same veil remains when the old covenant is read. It has not been
removed, because only in Christ is it taken away. Even to this
day when Moses is read, a veil covers their hearts. But whenever
anyone turns to the Lord, the VEIL IS TAKEN AWAY. Now the Lord
is the Spirit, and where the Spirit of the Lord is, there is freedom.
And we, who with UNVEILED FACES ALL REFLECT*

THE LORD'S GLORY, are being transformed into his likeness with ever-increasing glory, which comes from the Lord, who is the Spirit.
II Corinthians 3:13-18 – NIV

In this passage from Corinthians, we are dealing once again with the MIND of man, not the SOUL of man. Note that the MIND of man (at least in this passage) was made dull, not by sin, but by religion. The veil remains un-lifted under the religion and doctrines of Moses. But when one turns away from religion and turns toward God, the veil that exists as a result of the law is ultimately removed. Finally, we discover again the promise that we will reflect the image, likeness and even the glory of God.

THE ETERNAL CHRIST

For now we live in TIME. However, God lives in ETERNITY. God, who is simultaneously the *alpha and omega, beginning and end, first and last*, even *declaring the end from the beginning*, is more like a continuous eternal-cycle or eternal-circle than a linear time-line. So, in order to catch a glimpse into the ETERNAL MIND of God we must think outside the confines of time and past the boundaries of time-lines. We must think spherically, not linearly. And, we must welcome eternity into our limited time-space understanding.

In essence, the world was reconciled to God through Christ…IN ETERNITY… before this reconciliation ever showed up in TIME. Remember, the Lamb was slain *"before the foundation of the world." Revelation 13:8 – NKJV.* Allow me to say this in a more plain, less philosophical vernacular…

- Calvary is time's sitcom, but eternity's rerun -

In other words, when Jesus bore Calvary's cross in 33 A.D., He had already borne it eons prior in eternity. Jesus took on flesh *(in the fullness of time)* so that we could see IN TIME what has always been in eternity!

Perhaps Solomon tapped into a more inclusive and panoramic way of explaining this idea of Universal Salvation.

I know that whatever God does, it endures forever; nothing can be added to it nor anything taken from it. And God does it so that men will [reverently] fear Him [revere and worship Him, knowing that He is]. That which is now already has been, and that which is to be

> *already has been; and God seeks that which has passed by*
> *[so that history repeats itself].*
> **Ecclesiastes 3:14-15 - AMP**

Let us focus our attention on the phrase *That which IS NOW has already been*. In essence, what we wake up to in our *NOW* has always been so in the *IS* of God.

Consider the idea that God…

> …*WAS*, and *IS* and *IS TO COME*.
> **Revelation 1:4, 8; 4:8; 11:17**

Then, *I WAS SAVED*; *I AM SAVED*; and I am *BEING SAVED!*

I WAS SAVED…because the *Lamb was slain before the foundation of the world (Revelation 13)* and because *this grace was given to me in Christ Jesus before time began (II Timothy 1)*.

I AM SAVED…when I perceive (in time) this eternal truth - which leads me to *believe and confess (Romans 10)*.

I am BEING SAVED…as I grow in revelation and as I *CONTINUE to work out my own salvation with fear and trembling (Philippians 2:12)*. And, if I missed this revelation the first time around, God mercifully, spherically and providentially causes *history to repeat itself (Ecclesiastes 3:15)*.

Salvation is both timeless and continuous; instant and somehow a process; simultaneously finished and an ongoing work. In the mind of God, Salvation is eternal – no beginning and no ending. Yet, in the mind of the person receiving the revelation of salvation, it is happening for them at that very moment. Salvation was finished even before Jesus hung His head and declared *It Is Finished*. However, we are always working out our salvation.

Let us glean more understanding of this passage in Ecclesiastes 3 by reading it from the New International Version.

> *He has made everything beautiful in its time. He has also set eternity in the hearts of men; yet they cannot fathom what God has done from beginning to end. I know that everything God does will endure forever; nothing can be added to it and nothing taken from it. God does it so that men will revere him.*
> *Whatever is has already been, and what will be has been before; and God will call the past to account.*
> ***Ecclesiastes 3:11, 14-15 - NIV***

In this passage we see that God beautifies everything in *its time* – not in His! In God's time (or in eternity) all things are already beautiful. Even though we cannot see clearly into eternity, the eternal truths of God are set in our hearts. What is now a present reality for us in the time-space world has *already been*. And that which will happen in the future, has *been before*. In reference to the idea of Ultimate Reconciliation, the salvation that showed up when Jesus took on flesh – already existed before he came to earth!

The last part of this passage says *God will call the past to account*. The Amplified Bible says *God causes history to repeat itself.* In essence, Calvary has happened throughout time and will continue to happen so that the eternal truth of Christ may always have a presence in time as it does in eternity. It is with this thought in mind that we might begin to see salvation panoramically and begin to speak of salvation more inclusively – I *WAS* saved, I *AM* saved and I am *BEING* saved!

Blessed be the God and Father of our Lord Jesus Christ, who has blessed us with every spiritual blessing in the heavenly places in Christ, just as HE CHOSE US IN HIM BEFORE THE FOUNDATION OF THE WORLD, that we should be holy and without blame before Him in love, having PREDESTINED us to adoption as sons by Jesus Christ to Himself, according to the GOOD PLEASURE OF HIS WILL, to the praise of the glory of His grace, by which He made us accepted in the Beloved. In Him we have redemption through His blood, the forgiveness of sins, according to the riches of His grace which He made to abound toward us in all wisdom and prudence, having made known to us the mystery of HIS WILL, according to His good pleasure which He purposed in Himself, that in the dispensation of the FULLNESS OF THE TIMES He might gather together IN ONE ALL THINGS IN CHRIST, both which are in heaven and which are on earth— in Him. In Him also we have obtained an inheritance, being PREDESTINED according to the purpose of Him WHO WORKS ALL THINGS ACCORDING TO THE COUNSEL OF HIS WILL.
Ephesians 1:3-11 - NKJV

This passage in Ephesians is so full of Universalist doctrine. Let us take a closer look:

➤ We were chosen IN (the Eternal) CHRIST…BEFORE the Foundation of the world (again we did not choose Christ… we were chosen to be IN CHRIST).

➤ We were PREDESTINED to be adopted (or pre-appointed to be adopted through Christ as sons and daughters of God).

➤ This pre-choosing is the *Good Pleasure of God's Will* (remember it is *not the will of God that any one should perish* – and that *all things work according to the counsel of God's will*).

➢ We have been *made accepted* in the Beloved.

➢ God *made Grace abound toward us*.

➢ In TIME... *ALL THINGS* will be gathered into one, into Christ (even though they have already been gathered into Christ in Eternity).

Moreover, brethren, I do not want you to be unaware that all our fathers were under the cloud, all passed through the sea, all were baptized into Moses in the cloud and in the sea, all ate the same spiritual food, and all drank the same spiritual drink. For they drank of that spiritual Rock that followed them,
AND THAT ROCK WAS CHRIST.
I Corinthians 10:1-4 - NKJV

Paul is teaching here that (the Eternal) Christ was in the wilderness with the Israelites 1500 years before Jesus was born in Bethlehem. In other words, even before Jesus showed up in flesh, the intention, anointing and redemption that Jesus came to awaken us to already existed in the world, even if only in shadows and types. With regards to Universal salvation – the redeeming, saving spirit of (the Eternal) Christ has always been present in creation.

So do not be ashamed to testify about our Lord, or ashamed of me his prisoner. But join with me in suffering for the gospel, by the power of God, who has saved us and called us to a holy life—not because of anything we have done but because of his own purpose and grace. This GRACE WAS GIVEN US IN CHRIST JESUS BEFORE THE BEGINNING OF TIME, but it has NOW BEEN REVEALED THROUGH THE APPEARING of our Savior,

Christ Jesus, who has destroyed death and has brought life and immortality to light through the gospel.
II Timothy 1:8-10 - NIV

This passage in II Timothy reveals in a clear and irrefutable manner that grace was given to us in ETERNITY or *BEFORE THE BEGINNING OF TIME!* So, how do we become aware that we were given the grace of God by (the Eternal) Christ? We become aware that we have already been given grace through the APPEARING of Jesus *in the fullness* of TIME.

Even so we, when we were children, were in bondage under the elements of the world. But when the FULLNESS OF THE TIME had come, God sent forth His Son, born of a woman, born under the law, to redeem those who were under the law, that we might receive the adoption as sons.
Galatians 4:3-5 - NKJV

The Jesus "Person" shows up in TIME to reveal (the Eternal) Christ "Principle."

We do, however, speak a message of wisdom among the mature, but not the wisdom of this age or of the rulers of this age, who are coming to nothing. No, we speak of God's secret wisdom, a wisdom that has been hidden and that God destined for our glory before time began. None of the rulers of this age understood it, for if they had, they would not have crucified the Lord of glory.
However, as it is written:
"No eye has seen, no ear has heard, no mind has conceived what God has prepared for those who love him" but God has revealed it to us by his Spirit.

*The Spirit searches all things, even the deep things of God. For
who among men knows the thoughts of a man except the man's
spirit within him? In the same way no one knows the thoughts of
God except the Spirit of God. We have not received the spirit of the
world but the Spirit who is from God, that we may understand
what God has freely given us.*
I Corinthians 2:6-12 - NIV

The MYSTERY that has *been hidden* is now being revealed by
the Spirit of God.   And, what is the mystery being revealed? The
mystery being revealed is the hidden truth of what *God has freely
given us*... Salvation!

ALL IS CHRIST'S

One simple and clear way of explaining Universal Salvation from a scriptural standpoint is... if everything flows *from the Word* of God or from Christ, then everything is FROM Christ, OF Christ, IN Christ, BELONGS TO Christ - and everything ultimately will RETURN TO Christ. Consider these examples:

In the beginning was the Word, and the Word was with God, and the Word was God. He was with God in the beginning. THROUGH HIM ALL THINGS WERE MADE; WITHOUT HIM NOTHING WAS MADE THAT WAS MADE. The Word became flesh and made his dwelling among us. We have seen his glory, the glory of the One and Only, who came from the Father, full of grace and truth.
John 1:1-3, 14 - NIV

And he made known to us the mystery of his will according to his good pleasure, which he PURPOSED IN CHRIST, to be put into effect when the times will have reached their fulfillment—to bring ALL THINGS in heaven and on earth together UNDER ONE HEAD, EVEN CHRIST.
Ephesians 1:9-10 - NIV

When we consider these two verses (John 1:1-3, 14 and Ephesians 1:9-10) we find a powerful truth that not only shines a light on Universalist doctrine in the Bible, but we also discover a solid foundation on which we can build and support an eternal truth: EVERYTHING CAME FROM Christ...EVERYTHING WILL RETURN TO Christ.

I am the good shepherd; I know my sheep and my sheep know me—just as the Father knows me and I know the Father—and I lay down my life for the sheep. I HAVE OTHER SHEEP THAT ARE NOT OF THIS SHEEP PEN. I MUST BRING THEM ALSO. They too will listen to my voice, and there shall be ONE FLOCK and ONE SHEPHERD.
John 10:14-16 - NIV

To understand the power of this passage, and to apply it fully, we must look closely at the events surrounding it. The disciples have asked Jesus about a religious group that lived in Jesus' time, knew of His ministry and lived geographically in the same vicinity as Jesus (some speculate that this group were Hellenists). Yet, they were not disciples of Jesus, nor were they actively following Jesus. However, Jesus is so certain of His power to redeem and reclaim all of creation that He assures His disciples of this Universal Reconciliation by telling them that there are *sheep of other pastures* that belong to Him, but that they may not be presently following or even acknowledging Him. Then He declares to the disciples that He will *bring* these other sheep as well. Finally, He proclaims that there will be a unified flock under one shepherd. This confidence we see in Jesus flows from the eternal truth: EVERYTHING CAME FROM CHRIST...EVERYTHING WILL RETURN TO CHRIST (or in the mind of Jesus, "Everything came from Me...Everything will return to Me!")

In this next passage we stumble upon another occasion where the disciples ask Jesus again concerning a man who was not a part of their group but seemed to be doing good works and offering help to those in need. Once again Jesus shows confidence in knowing that even though this man may not have been a disciple and may not have been actively journeying with Him, Jesus knew this man was *in Christ*.

"Teacher," said John, "we saw a man driving out demons in your name and we told him to stop, because he was not one of us."
"Do not stop him," Jesus said. "No one who does a miracle in my name can in the next moment say anything bad about me, FOR WHOEVER IS NOT AGAINST US IS FOR US. I tell you the truth, anyone who gives you a cup of water in my name because you belong to Christ will certainly not lose his reward.
Mark 9:38-41 - NIV

Consider the *ALL* and the *EVERY* mentioned in the next several passages:

But I, when I am lifted up from the earth, will draw
ALL MEN to myself.
John 12:32 - NIV

That in (at) the name of Jesus EVERY knee should (MUST) bow, in heaven and on earth and under the earth, And EVERY tongue [frankly and openly] confess and acknowledge that Jesus Christ is Lord, to the glory of God the Father.
Philippians 2:10-11 - Amplified

He is the image of the invisible God, the firstborn over all creation. FOR BY HIM ALL THINGS WERE CREATED: things in heaven and on earth, visible and invisible, whether thrones or powers or rulers or authorities; ALL THINGS WERE CREATED BY HIM AND FOR HIM. He is before all things, and IN HIM ALL THINGS HOLD TOGETHER. And he is the head of the body, the church; he is the beginning and the firstborn from among the dead, so that in everything he might have the supremacy. For God was pleased to have all his fullness dwell in him, and through him to RECONCILE

TO HIMSELF ALL THINGS, whether things on earth or things in heaven, by making peace through his blood, shed on the cross.
Colossians 1:15-20 - NIV

Here (the mind being renewed in knowledge) there is no Greek or Jew, circumcised or uncircumcised, barbarian, Scythian, slave or free, but CHRIST IS ALL, and is IN ALL.
Colossians 3:11 - NIV

The declaration of Paul to the Colossians is *Christ IS ALL, and is IN ALL!* To fully grasp the magnitude of this statement we must be aware that the barbarians and Scythians had no contact with or knowledge of Jesus the Christ. These people groups did not yet even have an alphabet or recognized language. But, Paul declares that Christ is *in* them! How can Paul claim this about such people? Paul knows that all of creation must carry the DNA of the Creator!

But when it pleased God, who separated me from my mother's womb and called me through His grace, to reveal His Son IN ME, that I might preach Him among the Gentiles
Galatians 1:15-16 NKJV

Look closely at Paul's wording here in Galatians: *to reveal His Son IN ME* – not TO ME! In other words, Paul is declaring that Christ was already within him. But the Christ in Paul had to be uncovered or revealed. With Paul's personal understanding of the Christ that had always been in him he was able to write to the Colossians and proclaim that *Christ IS ALL and is IN ALL* (even in those who have never heard the name Jesus). As Paul journeyed throughout Gentile territory he began to use a very effective strategy. Paul did not preach Christ TO the Gentiles…rather he preached TO the Christ IN the Gentiles!

We have put our hope in the living God, who is the SAVIOR OF ALL PEOPLE, and especially of those who believe.
I Timothy 4:10 - NIV

Wow! Notice this Universalist declaration of God's salvation for ALL – *God, who is the savior of ALL people, and especially of those who believe.* Those who believe are saved. Those who do not believe are saved. But those who believe have connected their minds to what has already happened to their souls! That's why they are *especially* saved. Unbelievers are saved but UNAWARE. Believers are aware of or awakened to their salvation.

FAITH IN FAITH?

One of the most prevalent arguments against Universal Salvation is that man is a *free will agent* and therefore must respond to the free gift of Salvation with his own faith (or belief). Consider the next several passages that clearly show us that faith is not necessary to be reconciled to God (even though faith may be necessary to see and perceive that we have been reconciled to God).

> *What advantage then has the Jew, or what is the profit of circumcision? Much in every way! Chiefly because to them were committed the oracles of God. FOR WHAT IF SOME DID NOT BELIEVE? WILL THEIR UNBELIEF MAKE THE FAITHFULNESS OF GOD WITHOUT EFFECT? CERTAINLY NOT! Indeed, let God be true but every man a liar.*
> **Romans 3:1-4 - NKJV**

Here it is shown that man's lack of faith cannot thwart the plan of God or tamper with God's faithfulness. Then what is the advantage of believing and practicing faith? The advantage is that those who have faith and follow God will be trusted with the *oracles* or mysteries of the Word of God.

> *But because of his great love for us, God, who is rich in mercy, made us alive with Christ even when we were dead in transgressions—it is by grace you have been saved. And God raised us up with Christ and seated us with him in the heavenly realms in Christ Jesus, in order that in the coming ages he might show the incomparable riches of his grace, expressed in his kindness to us in Christ Jesus. For it is by grace you have been saved, through faith—and this NOT FROM YOURSELVES, IT IS THE GIFT OF GOD — not by works, so that no one can boast.*

FOR WE ARE GOD'S WORKMANSHIP, CREATED IN CHRIST JESUS TO DO GOOD WORKS, WHICH GOD PREPARED IN ADVANCE FOR US TO DO.
Ephesians 2:4-10 NKJV

Let us consider the phrase *by grace you have been saved, through faith.* Many would argue that we have been saved by the grace of God, but to really be saved we must respond in faith. Consider the very next statement *and this is not from yourselves, it is the gift of God.* Some would argue, yes, grace is a free gift but faith is required to receive the free gift. If something is free then there is no payment demanded or action required.

Allow me to point out here that grace does not come from us, and neither does faith initially come from us. Grace and Faith are gifts from God – lest any of us should try to boast in our grace or in our faith.

> ➢ Faith is not required for us to be reconciled to God.

> ➢ Faith is, however, required to fully realize that we have been reconciled to God through Christ.

> ➢ So, faith does not save us.

> ➢ Faith only connects our minds to the truth that we have already been saved!

Finally, we notice at the end of this particular passage that we are *God's workmanship, created IN CHRIST Jesus to do good works* (when?) *which God prepared IN ADAVANCE for us to do.* We were predestined to do good works and prepared for them in advance. We are the workmanship and handiwork of God. Jesus comes to uncover what has always been in us. As we continue to ponder these mysteries of faith let us be reminded that *we did not choose Christ... he chose us - John 15:16.*

One truth that must be considered as we struggle over these questions (Am I saved by my faith? Or by the Faithfulness of God and His Christ?) is the truth that Jesus is the *Author and Finisher* of OUR faith! Take a look at this passage in Hebrews in the New King James, Amplified and New International Versions.

...looking unto Jesus, the AUTHOR and FINISHER of our faith
Hebrews 12:2 NKJV

Looking away [from all that will distract] to Jesus, Who is the Leader and the Source of our faith [giving the first incentive for our belief] and is also its Finisher [bringing it to maturity and perfection].
Hebrews 12:2 – Amplified Bible

Let us fix our eyes on Jesus, the AUTHOR and PERFECTER of our faith, who for the joy set before him endured the cross, scorning its shame, and sat down at the right hand of the throne of God.
Hebrews 12:2 - NIV

So, we are saved by faith – but not by our faith! We are saved by the faith of Christ and the faithfulness of God. We cannot complete a completed work. We do not finish a finished work. We were created IN CHRIST to do GOOD WORKS...IN ADVANCE. Notice that the Amplified Version describes Jesus even *giving the first incentive for our belief* and then *bringing it to perfection*. We should all believe in Christ and have our own faith – while recognizing that we would not even know how to begin to have our own faith had Jesus not given us *the first incentive*!

Notice how the Amplified Bible clearly explains this relationship of man's will and strength being secondary to God's will and strength. And further, that even man's desire to turn toward God is not his own, but placed there and energized by God.

[Not in your own strength] FOR IT IS GOD ALL THE WHILE EFFECTUALLY AT WORK IN YOU [energizing and CREATING IN YOU the power and desire], BOTH TO WILL AND TO WORK for His good pleasure and satisfaction and delight.
Philippians 2:13 - AMP

All of humanity should, and will, confess and surrender to the knowledge of God and His Christ. However, we must be cognizant of the truth that we do not come to confession or to surrender of our own accord.

Now let us ask a very obvious question: If the world is saved…what is the purpose of faith? Here is a very simple answer: FAITH is the KEY to UNDERSTANDING Salvation (not the key to salvation)! Faith is the key to the comprehension and realization of salvation, not the key to receiving salvation. Our faith only allows us to realize the faithfulness of God and the finished work of Christ. Allow me to say it this way – My SOUL is saved by the Faith OF Christ, but my MIND is saved (or put at ease) by my Faith IN Christ. Faith unlocks the mystery and allows us access to see the faithfulness of our God. Faith enables us to stand in TIME and peek into ETERNITY. Remember, Jesus AUTHORS (initiates) our faith and FINISHES (perfects and matures) our faith!

THE WILL OF GOD? OR THE WILL OF MAN?

Is the FINAL OUTCOME of man (and the universe) dependent upon MAN'S WILL? Or the WILL of GOD? Many hold to the concept that God cannot and will not supersede the will of man, nor superimpose His will on, in or through man. If God has lost control of man and the universe, then how does God *declare the END of a matter from the BEGINNING?* Could it be that God *works ALL THINGS according to the COUNSEL OF HIS WILL?*

Consider these verses in Romans where we clearly find the hidden truth that God is truly providential in His dealing with humanity:

What shall we say then? Is there unrighteousness with God? Certainly not! For He says to Moses, "I will have mercy on whomever I will have mercy, and I will have compassion on whomever I will have compassion." So then it is NOT OF HIM WHO WILLS, nor of him who runs, BUT OF GOD WHO SHOWS MERCY. For the Scripture says to the Pharaoh, "For this very purpose I have raised you up, that I may show My power in you, and that My name may be declared in all the earth." Therefore HE HAS MERCY ON WHOM HE WILLS, and whom He wills He hardens. You will say to me then, "WHY DOES HE STILL FIND FAULT? FOR WHO HAS RESISTED HIS WILL?" But indeed, O man, who are you to reply against God? Will the thing formed say to him who formed it, "Why have you made me like this?" DOES NOT THE POTTER HAVE POWER OVER THE CLAY, FROM THE SAME LUMP TO MAKE ONE VESSEL FOR HONOR AND ANOTHER FOR DISHONOR? What if God, wanting to show His wrath and to make His power known, ENDURED WITH MUCH LONGSUFFERING THE VESSELS OF WRATH PREPARED FOR DESTRUCTION, and that He might make known the riches of His glory on the vessels of mercy, which He had prepared beforehand

*for glory, even us whom He called, not of the Jews only,
but also of the Gentiles?
As He says also in Hosea:
" I will call them My people, who were not My people, And her
beloved, who was not beloved. And it shall come to pass in the
place where it was said to them, ' You are not My people,' There
they shall be called sons of the living God."*
Romans 9:14-26 NKJV

*What then shall we say? Is God unjust? Not at all! For he says
to Moses, "I will have mercy on whom I have mercy, and I will
have compassion on whom I have compassion." IT DOES NOT,
THEREFORE, DEPEND ON MAN'S DESIRE OR EFFORT,
BUT ON GOD'S MERCY.*
Romans 9:14-16 NIV

Notice that *God SHOWS MERCY on whomever HE WILLS* and also *HARDENS whomever HE WILLS*. And all of it is working together in the providential plan of God. Even the wicked ruler Pharaoh is in the hand of God (God hardening Pharaoh in order to *show forth His power*, and to *declare His name in all the earth*). Paul then asks the obvious question – If God hardened Pharaoh's heart for His own purpose…does God *still find fault* with Pharaoh *FOR WHO HAS RESISTED (or can resist) HIS WILL*? Then comes the answer – God makes some *vessels for honor* and some *vessels for dishonor*! And further, the *vessels of dishonor* should not question or *reply against God* for the way they were *formed*.

Also, pay very close attention to the idea in this passage where Paul declares it is *not of him who WILLS, nor of him who RUNS* (or resists) *but of GOD WHO SHOWS MERCY*! In other words, the will of man matters not.

Whether man agrees with God or resists…God's will shall prevail. The New International Version says *IT DOES NOT, THEREFORE, DEPEND ON MAN'S DESIRE OR EFFORT.*

Only two chapters later in the book of Romans we uncover even more of the unfolding providence of God where He declares that even those who were made for dishonor will ultimately be shown mercy.

FOR THE GIFTS AND CALLING OF GOD ARE IRREVOCABLE.
For as you were once disobedient to God, yet have NOW
OBTAINED MERCY THROUGH THEIR DISOBEDIENCE,
even so these also have now been disobedient, that through the
mercy shown you they also may obtain mercy. FOR GOD HAS
COMMITED THEM ALL TO DISOBEDIENCE,
that He might have MERCY ON ALL.
Oh, the depth of the riches both of the wisdom and knowledge of
God! How unsearchable are His judgments and
His ways past finding out!
" For who has known the mind of the LORD? Or who has become
His counselor?" Or who has first given to Him
And it shall be repaid to him?"
For OF HIM and THROUGH HIM and TO HIM are ALL
THINGS, to whom be glory forever. Amen.
Romans 11:28-36 NKJV

Here Paul proclaims the *GIFTS AND CALLING OF GOD ARE IRREVOCABLE.* This very statement is made in the context of and in reference to those who were being disobedient. In other words, God *gifts, calls* and even casts some to play a role of being disobedient in order to shine a light on the virtues of being obedient (*i.e.* – *NOW OBTAINED MERCY THROUGH THEIR DISOBEDIENCE*). Paul goes even further to describe that God *COMMITED THEM ALL TO*

DISOBEDIENCE that He might have MERCY ON ALL (the Amplified Bible says "God SHUT THEM ALL UP IN DISOBEDIENCE").

In the end, God will have mercy on ALL! Our human drama clouds our ability to understand the *judgments and ways* of God. However, whether we understand how it all works or not, there are a few things of which we can be sure – it's all *OF HIM* and working *THROUGH HIM* and answering *TO HIM* and ultimately God will get the glory!

Man can, however, attempt to resist or fight against the providential will of God. But in the end, man's power to RESIST is not as great as God's providence to REDEEM! Saul of Tarsus (who would later become the Apostle Paul) attempted to resist the will of God, and did for a season. Yet, Saul's will to resist was no match for God's will to redeem! Here is the question God asks Saul while He was confronting him and ultimately redirecting his destiny and direction:

And he said, "Who are You, Lord?" Then the Lord said, "I am Jesus, whom you are persecuting. It is hard for you to kick against the goads."
Acts 9:5 and 26:14 - NKJV

The Amplified Bible records that God asks Saul why do you *keep offering VAIN and perilous RESISTANCE*. The New Living Translation puts it this way - *It is USELESS FOR YOU TO FIGHT AGAINST MY WILL.*

(Who else is a God like You...) Declaring the END from the BEGINNING, And from ancient times things that are not yet done, Saying, 'MY COUNSEL SHALL STAND, AND I WILL DO ALL MY PLEASURE.
Isaiah 46:10 - NKJV

The reason God can *declare the end from the beginning* is because God knows the ultimate outcome – and God *will do all of His pleasure.* In other words, God *WORKS ALL THINGS ACCORDING TO THE COUNSEL OF HIS WILL!*

Being predestined according to the purpose of Him who works
all things according to the counsel of His will,
Ephesians 1:11 - NKJV

The FINAL OUTCOME of man, of the universe and of the creation is not left up to chance. If it is the will of God that *no man should perish* and *God works all things according to the counsel of His will*, how can anything besides the Ultimate Reconciliation of all of humanity back to God even be in the realm of possibility? However, the pace at which we both progress toward our divinity and the space in which we surrender to God's will may be left up to us…at least for a season.

ATONEMENT MADE FOR ALL

*This is to be a lasting ordinance for you: Atonement is to be made
once a year for ALL THE SINS of the Israelites."*
Leviticus 16:34 - NIV

The one paschal lamb which was offered as a sacrifice for the sins
of the Israelites was offered once a year for ALL of the Israelites.
However, it is imperative to remember there were several million
Israelites. There is no feasible way that each Israelite could schedule
a meeting with the High Priest to repent and ask forgiveness. So one
sacrifice was offered for the atonement and for the redemption of
ALL! In this same manner, through the finished work of Christ –
ALL OF THE WORLD is atoned for.

*My dear children, I write this to you so that you will not sin. But
if anybody does sin, we have one who speaks to the Father in
our defense—Jesus Christ, the Righteous One. He is the atoning
sacrifice for our sins, AND NOT ONLY FOR OURS BUT ALSO
FOR THE SINS OF THE WHOLE WORLD.*
I John 2:1-2 - NIV

Paul includes not only the believing Christians and Jews in the
Atonement, but he also says that Jesus made atonement for the
WHOLE WORLD!

*But I, when I am lifted up from the earth, will draw
ALL MEN to myself.*
John 12:32 - NIV

The next day John saw Jesus coming toward him and said, "Look, the LAMB OF GOD, who takes away the SIN OF THE WORLD!"
John 1:29 - NIV

When John the Baptist declares of Jesus that he *takes away the sin of the world* he is actually and more accurately saying that Jesus takes away the *offense* of the world. The Greek word used here for sin is *hamartia* – meaning *offense*. So, because of the atoning work of Christ, the world, and its sin, no longer offends God. However, a second Greek word for sin is *hamartano* – meaning *to miss the mark*. This use of the word sin is found in this next verse.

My little children, these things I write to you, so that you may not sin. And if anyone sins, we have an Advocate with the Father, Jesus Christ the righteous. And He Himself is the propitiation for our sins, and not for ours only but also for the whole world.
I John 2:1-2 NKJV

Because of the atoning work of Christ, the Lamb of God who takes away the sin *(hamartia / offense)* of the world, we can no longer offend God. Yet, we can still fall short *(hamartano / miss the mark)*. But, when we do fall short, we have an advocate speaking on our behalf; our elder brother, Jesus the Christ.

BE CAUTIOUS OF THE "ELDER BROTHER" SYNDROME

Let us be self-aware or self-examining regarding the goodness and ALLNESS of God's love and power to reconcile. For instance, in the story of the Prodigal Son, the elder brother becomes upset when his younger brother returns to the Father's House and is immediately celebrated and treated like royalty.

But the father said to his servants, 'Quick! Bring the best robe and put it on him. Put a ring on his finger and sandals on his feet. Bring the fattened calf and kill it. Let's have a feast and celebrate. For this son of mine was dead and is alive again; he was lost and is found.' So they began to celebrate. Meanwhile, the older son was in the field. When he came near the house, he heard music and dancing. So he called one of the servants and asked him what was going on. 'Your brother has come,' he replied, 'and your father has killed the fattened calf because he has him back safe and sound.'
THE OLDER BROTHER BECAME ANGRY AND REFUSED TO GO IN.
Luke 15:22-28 - NIV

Remember, Jesus said of the Pharisees (those who believed they had to earn salvation through works) that they *stand at the door... they will not enter and will not allow others to enter.* Those who have the mission and harbor the mentality of keeping others out never realize they themselves have not entered. Furthermore, the reason many believers become so upset with the ideas of Ultimate Reconciliation is because they feel they are laboring in vain or that somehow someone else will receive the same reward for doing less work.

So his father went out and pleaded with him. But he answered his father, 'Look! All these years I've been slaving for you and never disobeyed your orders. Yet you never gave me even a young goat so I could celebrate with my friends. But when this son of yours who has squandered your property with prostitutes comes home, you kill the fattened calf for him!'
Luke 15:28-30 - NIV

Be mindful of three things at this point. 1) In the kingdom the *last will be first and the greatest will be as a servant.* Also, remember that those who come in at the "eleventh hour" receive the same reward as those who labored all day. 2) Try to realize that those of us who have been laboring faithfully in the field for the Father have avoided the present-hell that is a consequence of disobedience, and that we have bypassed many of the painful "hog-pens of life." Most importantly, realize that we have been privileged to enjoy the Father's Presence or experience abundant life and the Kingdom of God here and now in this earthly lifetime. 3) Many believers adopt an exclusive mindset because they are ignorant of what the Father has already given to them! Consider the words of the Father to the elder brother:

'My son,' the father said, 'YOU ARE ALWAYS WITH ME, and EVERYTHING I HAVE IS YOURS.'
Luke 15:31 – NIV

There is no cause to be jealous or angry. Everything is already ours. Our mentality should be a Kingdom Mentality… that if we will seek first the Kingdom of God… all of our needs will be met… and we will be given the Kingdom in this lifetime… now!

But seek the kingdom of God, and all these things
shall be added to you.
"Do not fear, little flock, for it is your Father's good pleasure
to give you the kingdom."
Luke 12:31-32 - NIV

THE ALLNESS OF GOD IN THE OLD TESTAMENT

In order to show a consistent pattern and a constant current of Universalist Doctrine and scripture throughout the entire Bible, allow me to present an exhaustive number of references of the All-Inclusive nature of God as seen in the Old Testament.

Now the LORD had said to Abram: "Get out of your country, From your family And from your father's house, To a land that I will show you. I will make you a great nation; I will bless you and make your name great; And you shall be a blessing.
I will bless those who bless you, And I will curse him who curses you; And in you ALL THE FAMILIES IN THE EARTH shall be blessed."
Genesis 12:1-3 - NKJV

ALL NATIONS of the earth will be blessed in you… through your offspring.
Genesis 18:18; 22:18; 26:4; Psalm 72:17; Galatians 3:8

The glory of the Lord appeared to ALL the people.
Leviticus 9:23 - NIV

As surely as I live and as surely as the glory of the LORD fills THE WHOLE EARTH.
Numbers 14:21 - NIV

But Moses and Aaron fell facedown and cried out, "O God, God of the spirits of ALL MANKIND, will you be angry with the entire assembly when only one man sins?"
Numbers 16:22 - NIV

May the LORD, the God of the spirits of ALL MANKIND, appoint a man over this community.
Numbers 27:16 - NIV

To the LORD your God belong the heavens, even the highest heavens, the earth and everything in it.
Deuteronomy 10:14 - NIV

Like water spilled on the ground, which cannot be recovered, so we must die. But God does not take away life; instead, HE DEVISES WAYS so that a banished person may not remain estranged from him.
II Samuel 14:14 - NIV

The true heart of God is found here in this passage in II Samuel – God *DEVISES WAYS* to gather and reconcile even a *banished* and *estranged* person.

Yours, O LORD, is the greatness and the power and the glory and the majesty and the splendor, for EVERYTHING IN HEAVEN AND EARTH IS YOURS. Yours, O LORD, is the kingdom; you are exalted as HEAD OVER ALL. Wealth and honor come from you; you are the RULER OF ALL THINGS. In your hands are strength and power to exalt and GIVE STRENGTH TO ALL.
I Chronicles 29:11-12 - NIV

O LORD, God of our fathers, are you not the God who is in heaven? You rule over ALL THE KINGDOMS of the nations. Power and might are in your hand, and no one can withstand you.
II Chronicles 20:5 - NIV

You alone are the LORD. You made the heavens, even the highest heavens, and all their starry host, the earth and all that is on it, the seas and all that is in them. YOU GIVE LIFE TO EVERYTHING, and the multitudes of heaven worship you.
Nehemiah 9:6 - NIV

Which of all these does not know that the hand of the LORD has done this?
In his hand is the life of EVERY CREATURE and the breath of ALL MANKIND. To him belong strength and victory; both DECEIVED AND DECEIVER ARE HIS (Amplified says "deceived and deceiver are His and in His power").
Job 12:9-10, 16 – NIV

In this passage from Job the *DECEIVED and (even the) DECEIVER* are His!

ALL THE ENDS OF THE EARTH will remember and turn to the LORD, and ALL THE FAMILIES OF THE NATIONS will bow down before him, for dominion belongs to the LORD and he rules over the nations. All the rich of the earth will feast and worship; all who go down to the dust will kneel before him those who cannot keep themselves alive.
Psalm 22:27-29 - NIV

THE EARTH IS THE LORD'S, AND EVERYTHING IN IT,
THE WORLD, AND ALL WHO LIVE IN IT.
Psalm 24:1 - NIV

ALL KINGS will bow down to him and all nations will serve him.
May his name endure forever; may it continue as long as the sun.
ALL NATIONS will be blessed through him, and they will call him
blessed. Praise be to the LORD God, the God of Israel, who alone
does marvelous deeds. Praise be to his glorious name forever;
MAY THE WHOLE EARTH BE FILLED WITH HIS GLORY.
Amen and Amen.
Psalm 72:11, 17-19 - NIV

I said, You are "gods"; YOU ARE ALL SONS of the Most High.
But you will die like mere men; you will fall like every other ruler.
Rise up, O God, judge the earth, for ALL THE NATIONS
ARE YOUR INHERITANCE.
Psalm 82:6-8 - NIV

The LORD has established his throne in heaven,
and HIS KINGDOM RULES OVER ALL.
Psalm 103:19 – NIV

In the last days the mountain of the LORD'S temple will be
established as chief among the mountains; it will be raised above
the hills, and ALL NATIONS WILL STREAM TO IT.
Isaiah 2:2 - NIV

And the glory of the LORD will be revealed, and ALL MANKIND
TOGETHER will see it. For the mouth of the LORD has spoken.
Isaiah 40:5 - NIV

I am the LORD, and there is NO OTHER; APART FROM ME THERE IS NO GOD. I will strengthen you, though you have not acknowledged me, so that from the rising of the sun to the place of its setting men may know THERE IS NONE BESIDES ME. I am the LORD, and THERE IS NO OTHER. I form the light and create darkness, I bring prosperity and create disaster; I, the LORD, do all these things. By myself I have sworn, my mouth has uttered in all integrity a word that will not be revoked: Before me EVERY KNEE WILL BOW; BY ME EVERY TONGUE WILL SWEAR. They will say of me, 'In the LORD alone are righteousness and strength.' ALL WHO HAVE RAGED AGAINST HIM WILL COME TO HIM and be put to shame.
Isaiah 45:5-7, 23-24 - NIV

The Amplified adds further clarification to this verse: *Unto Me every knee will bow and every tongue will SWEAR ALLEGIANCE to Him... ONLY IN THE LORD shall one say, I HAVE RIGHTEOUSNESS (SALVATION AND VICTORY) and strength [to achieve]. To Him shall all come who were incensed against Him, and they shall be ashamed.*

This is the covenant I will make with the house of Israel after that time, declares the LORD. "I will put my law in their minds and write it on their hearts. I will be their God, and they will be my people. NO LONGER WILL A MAN TEACH HIS NEIGHBOR, OR A MAN HIS BROTHER, SAYING, 'KNOW THE LORD', BECAUSE THEY WILL ALL KNOW ME, FROM THE LEAST OF THEM TO THE GREATEST," declares the Lord. "FOR I WILL FORGIVE THEIR WICKEDNESS AND WILL REMEMBER THEIR SINS NO MORE."
Jeremiah 31:33-34 - NIV

FOR MEN ARE NOT CAST BY THE LORD FOREVER. Though he brings grief, he will show compassion, so great is his unfailing love. For he does not willingly bring affliction or grief to the children of men. To crush underfoot all prisoners in the land, to deny a man his rights before the Most High, to deprive a man of justice — would not the Lord see such things?
Lamentations 3:31-36 - NIV

The word of the LORD came to me: "What do you people mean by quoting this proverb about the land of Israel: 'The fathers eat sour grapes and the children's teeth are set on edge'? As surely as I live, declares the Sovereign LORD, you will no longer quote this proverb in Israel. FOR EVERY LIVING SOUL BELONGS TO ME, the father as well as the son —both alike belong to me.
Ezekiel 18:1-4 - NIV

In my vision at night I looked, and there before me was one like a son of man, coming with the clouds of heaven. He approached the Ancient of Days and was led into his presence. He was given authority, glory and sovereign power; ALL PEOPLES, NATIONS AND MEN OF EVERY LANGUAGE WORSHIPED HIM. His dominion is an everlasting dominion that will not pass away, and his kingdom is one that will never be destroyed.
Daniel 7:13-14 - NIV

In the place where it was said to them, 'You are not my people,' they will be called 'sons of the living God.'
Hosea 1:10 - NIV

And afterward, I will pour out my Spirit on ALL PEOPLE. Your sons and daughters will prophesy, your old men will dream dreams, your young men will see visions.

*Even on my servants, both men and women, I will pour out
my Spirit in those days.*
Joel 2:28-29 - NIV

*In the last days the mountain of the LORD'S temple will be
established as chief among the mountains; it will be raised above
the hills and ALL PEOPLES will stream to it. Many nations
will come and say, "Come, let us go up to the mountain of the
LORD, to the house of the God of Jacob. He will teach us his ways,
so that we may walk in his paths." He will judge between many
peoples and will settle disputes for strong nations far and wide.
They will beat their swords into plowshares and their spears into
pruning hooks. NATION WILL NOT TAKE UP SWORD AGAINST
NATION, NOR WILL THEY TRAIN FOR WAR ANYMORE.*
Micah 4:1-3 - NIV

*For the earth will be filled with the knowledge of the glory of the
LORD, as the waters cover the sea.*
Habakkuk 2:14 - NIV

*My name will be great among the nations, from the rising to the
setting of the sun. In EVERY PLACE incense and pure offerings
will be brought to my name, because my name will be great
AMONG THE NATIONS, says the LORD Almighty.*
Malachi 1:11 – NIV

REVIEW

As we close this section on Universal Salvation let us take with us some basic scriptural truths and clear statements that will provide us a biblical foundation that substantiates a Christian adherence to and teaching of this doctrine:

➤ IF ALL MEN DIED IN ADAM…ALL MEN WILL LIVE IN CHRIST (*Romans 5:10-11, 14, 18; I Corinthians 15:21-22*). Jesus' finished work of life and obedience is NOT LESS POWERFUL or less complete than Adam's work of death and disobedience. Death was imputed to all through Adam…Life is imputed to all through Christ.

➤ Universal Salvation is not a LAST DAYS false teaching; is not a NEW DOCTRINE; and does not lack SOUND BIBLICAL FOUNDATION. Universal Salvation is as ancient as Christianity and nearly as old as the Bible itself (*refer to Early Church Fathers Origen, St. Jerome, Gregory of Nyssa and Clement of Alexandria*).

➤ The SOUL of man has been reconciled to God through Christ (even if the MIND of man is unaware of this reconciliation - *Colossians 1:15-22*).

➤ God's ETERNAL plan of Universal Salvation was in place long before man ever sinned, and even before Jesus shows up in TIME. Yet, *in the fullness of TIME*, Jesus comes to earth to reveal the ETERNAL plan of God (*II Timothy 1:8-10*).

➤ EVERYTHING came FROM Christ...EVERYTHING will RETURN back TO Christ (*John 1:1-3, 14; Ephesians 1:9-10*). If ALL of creation came from Christ, then ALL of creation belongs to Christ.

➤ FAITH is not necessary for man to be reconciled to God. However, FAITH is necessary for man to become aware of his being reconciled to God (*Romans 3:1-4; Ephesians 2:4-10; Hebrews 12:2*). Jesus is the AUTHOR and FINISHER of our faith. I am saved by faith, but not by my faith. I am saved through the faithfulness of God and His Christ. My SOUL is saved by the Faith of Christ. Yet, my MIND is saved (or awakened) by my Faith in Christ.

The Holy Bible of Inclusion

Part III – THE DEVIL

———◆———

-A GOD Perspective of the DEVIL-
*

-The Hebrew and Greek devil-
*

-Satan the Idea (not the Individual)-
*

-The devil made me do it-
*

-God or devil? G(O)OD OR (D)EVIL?-
*

-It's All God (dispelling Duality)-
*

-No Other God (Not even the devil)-
*

-If God is All there is…-
*

-How to Deal with the devil-
*

A GOD PERSPECTIVE OF THE DEVIL

The devil has become a very valued part of Christianity and church culture all across the globe. Most Christians blame the devil for our bad behavior, our lack of self-discipline, and for our poor choices. But this can no longer be a luxury when we know better. Very few Christian church services, if any, are devoid of the presence of the devil due to the recognition he is given in them. In many church services the devil is mentioned and focused upon even more than Jesus. No wonder non-Christians are confused by people who say they love Jesus more than anything yet talk about the devil twice as much. So, if the devil is, and seemingly must be, a part of our church culture, then we ought to understand more deeply the role and purpose of the devil.

Interestingly enough, most of what Christendom believes, or has adopted, regarding Satan was incorporated into the Bible from other sources. For example, the image of Satan as a forked-tailed, horned demon with a goat's body is derived from descriptions of the Greek god *Pan* and not from the original Hebrew scripture.

Before we can accurately understand actual biblical concepts about the devil, we must know where they have come from in order to gain a PROPER PERSPECTIVE; especially when speaking or thinking of the devil in comparison to God. Let us begin by acknowledging that Satan, or *the devil*, IS NOT – and never will nor can be – the exact, opposite equal to God! It is from an ancient religion known as Zoroastrianism that Christianity borrows the belief of a good god and an evil god battling each other with equal power. From this concept the idea has taken shape that the devil is just as powerful as God. And in fact, those who subscribe to the belief that Christianity is the ONLY way to God would be forced to admit that presently (according to this way of thinking) the devil is winning this battle because only approximately 1.5 billion of the world's 7 billion people claim to be Christians.

Belief in and about the devil can become a very divisive topic. Therefore, in an effort to promote unity in the Body of Christ, let us remember that each person interprets the Bible and its truth differently - specifically in regards to hell or evil or (d)evil. But, if we can only agree that our God has no equal, and is the all-powerful creative force in the universe, then we have found ample common ground upon which we can stand and reason together.

Finally, we are BELIEVERS! So, let us not allow our focus to be centered on NOT BELIEVING in the devil or his hell. But rather, let us declare that we BELIEVE IN a God who is all-powerful!

For instance, I believe the devil or (d)evil exists.
However, I believe IN God or Ultimate G(o)od!

THE HEBREW AND GREEK DEVIL

The Hebrew name Satan (pronounced *say-tawn*) actually means "adversary." The Greek for devil (pronounced *diabolos*) is also translated as "adversary" and is at times used as a proper name for anything that opposes God.

For example, in *I Samuel 29:4*, the Hebrew word for "Satan" is used to indicate a potential HUMAN ADVERSARY in the Philistine Army – not the devil.

And, in this next passage, the Hebrew word *saytawn* (Satan or adversary) is used in the context of two kings that GOD RAISES UP to be Solomon's adversaries.

> *And the LORD stirred up an adversary (satan) unto Solomon,*
> *Hadad the Edomite: he was of the king's seed in Edom… And*
> *God stirred him up another adversary (satan), Rezon the son of*
> *Eliadah, which fled from his lord Hadadezer king of Zobah.*
> **I Kings 11:14, 23 - KJV**

Notice in this next passage that the ANGEL OF THE LORD is called an adversary or "Satan" when he blocks the path of Balaam.

> *Then God's anger was aroused because he went, and the ANGEL*
> *OF THE LORD took His stand in the way as an ADVERSARY*
> *(satan) against him… And the Angel of the LORD said to him,*
> *"Why have you struck your donkey these three times? Behold, I*
> *have come out to stand against you, because*
> *your way is perverse before Me."*
> **Numbers 22:22, 32 – NKJV**

Consider this question: If Satan or Adversary is referred to as *THE ANGEL OF THE LORD*...how does Satan operate outside the control, purpose, power and will of God?

Another name used for Satan / (d)evil in the scriptures is *LUCIFER*.

(Interesting Note: the name *LUCIFER* comes from a Latin translation of *Isaiah 14:12* in which the Babylonian king is linked to a fallen Morning Star, *lucerne ferre* or "bearer of light.")

SATAN THE IDEA (not the INDIVIDUAL)

Most often in the Bible, the assigning of the name or usage of Satan (*saytawn or diablos* – meaning *adversary*) is not referencing an actual BEING, PERSON, PERSONA or INDIVIDUAL, but rather in reference to an object, an obstacle or an IDEA (such as sickness, poverty or anything seemingly standing in the way of our advancing on the journey of realizing more of God's purposes in the earth and in our own lives).

For instance, Jesus calls Peter the "Rock," and on his revelation of *the Christ*, Jesus declares that the church will be built and that the gates of hell would not be able to prevail against it. But, not long after this praise for Peter Jesus rebukes him and then calls him "Satan" for standing in the way of His destiny on the cross of Calvary! Had Peter actually become Satan? Or was Jesus simply suggesting that Peter's action of standing in the way of His destiny at Calvary was adversarial to the purposes of God?

Can we assign a "Persona" (personage or personality) to the (d)evil?

Based on this understanding of the name Satan, anything that acts as an adversary to our realization of the abundant life can be perceived as a devil. However, these adversaries and obstacles are not to be compared with and are no match for the all-powerful, all-knowing God that we serve!

There is nothing harmful in calling a sickness or a disease "Satan" and then speaking against it or "casting it out." However, personifying the idea of "adversary" in the form of a SPECIFIC BEING who according to present day Christian belief supposedly claims 70% of God's children for hell, while God is only gathering about 30% of His children for heaven, is just one example of the misuse and DANGER of this misdirected assignation of a god-like persona to a being who is somehow (at least in Christian circles) often thought of as being almost equal in power to God.

As I referenced earlier, many scholars attribute Satan's development and growth from an adversary to the "archenemy" of God, to the influence of the Persian religion, Zoroastrianism, which contains a concept similar to *Star Wars*, in which two opposing forces – one good and the other evil – struggle for ultimate control of the universe. However, the Old Testament's notion of Satan as being inferior to God and needing to receive permission from God before "raising hell" on earth (as in the story of Job) can also be found in the New Testament where the role of Satan seems at times to be a bit magnified.

And the Lord said, "Simon, Simon! Indeed, Satan has ASKED for you, that he may sift you as wheat. But I have prayed for you, that your faith should not fail; and when you have returned to Me, strengthen your brethren."
Luke 22:31-32 - NKJV

Notice that Satan had to ASK God permission in regards to Peter. Just as with Job, God used the devil or evil for His own purposes, but He set the parameters.

Then Jesus WAS LED (guided) BY THE HOLY SPIRIT into the wilderness (desert) TO BE TEMPTED (tested and tried) BY THE DEVIL.
Matthew 4:1 - AMP

Let's paraphrase the previous verse – *Then Jesus was led by the Spirit... to the devil!* When you study the events that occur immediately after this encounter with the devil you find that Jesus has come into a new sense of power and a new season of anointing. Does this scripture imply that Jesus' moment of testing, tempting, or better still preparation with the devil serves to ultimately release His power and reveal His Person? It would seem so.

The *Khaboris Manuscript* (an ancient Aramaic collection of the Gospels) reveals to us that Jesus was not at all with any devil or even evil – but alone with his *own temptations* working through His humanity and becoming divine. Because it is in the original language Jesus spoke, this translation could and should actually be considered more original or accurate than the Greek translations of the Gospels. In it we also see that Jesus was not being tempted or tortured by a devil – but was being prepared and propelled into the full awareness of His divinity by what is referred to in this Aramaic manuscript, not as the devil, but as *Uprightness!*

Here is **Matthew 4:1-8** from the *Khaboris Manuscript*:

*v.1 - Then Jesus was drawn from (min) rukha d'koodsha into an unprotected state (madbra) for what would be His stress from **UPRIGHTNESS** (adhilkarrsa).*

v.2 - And he fasted forty days and forty nights. At the end He hungered.

*v.3 - and then came **HIS OWN TEMPTATIONS** (damanasii) and said to Him, "If You are the Son of God (Alaha) say to these stones to become bread."*

v.4 - But He responded and said, "It is written that not by bread alone does a man have a perfect life (khayi), but by every word (mila) that issues from the mouth of God (Alaha)."

*v.5 - Then **UPRIGHTNESS** (adhilkarrsa) carried Him to a holy (koodsha) city and stood Him upon the pinnacle of the temple.*

v.6 - and said to Him, "If You are the Son of God, cast Your napsha (napshak) down. For it is written His angels will have charge of you, and on their hands they will take you, so that your feet will not be touched by stone."

*v.7 - Jesus said to **IT**, "Also it is written to put not the Lord your God to a test."*

*v.8 - Again **UPRIGHTNESS** (adhilkarrsa) carried Him to a very high mountain and pointed out for Him all the kingdoms of the world and their glories...*

Let us focus on several key Aramaic words that contain incredible revelation about the "devil" from the *Khaboris Manuscript:*

➢ In verses 1,5, and 8 we find that the devil, or this agent of temptation, is not thought of as evil, but as a means of guiding Jesus to a higher place of consciousness. Thus, in Aramaic, is referred to as *UPRIGHTNESS!* All of the English translations of this verse would confirm this idea as they paint the picture that Jesus was *LED by the Spirit TO THE DEVIL.* If nothing good can come from the devil... why would the Spirit lead Jesus to the devil? Because the devil (Uprightness) plays a necessary role in awakening a certain part of Jesus – and us!

➢ In verse 3 we find another very provocative revelation. The Khaboris Manuscript purports to us that Jesus was not even being tempted by an outside force – but merely being tested by an inner voice. Thus, *and then came HIS OWN TEMPTATIONS and said to Him.* In other words, the divine in Jesus was confronting and conversing with the human in Jesus. We find a similar example of this as Jesus was pleading "with God" in the Garden of Gethsemane. In this moment of intense prayer and introspection, Jesus confronts once and for all any remaining shred of His own humanity that would attempt to keep Him from His divine purpose, and from His divine person. If we accept the idea that Jesus was, and IS God, then we must accept that Jesus was, at least in some sense, talking to Himself in the Garden of Gethsemane! This inner conversation that began in the desert with Himself – not the devil – continued and concluded in the garden.

➤ Notice finally in verse 7 that the devil or Satan or Uprightness is not an INDIVIDUAL, but an IDEA. Thus, this Aramaic translation reads *Jesus said to IT* (not to him). *IT* is not a person or even a personification. *IT* is an idea! The devil is not present during this necessary moment of transition and transformation in Jesus' life. However, *IT* is present. The IDEA and IDEAL was present. And, *IT* was leading and guiding Jesus to confront His humanity, His pride, His flesh – as *IT* was being used of God to push Jesus into His destiny as the Christ.

So, it was the devil that caused Jesus to deal with Himself and to ultimately conquer His own human will? Perhaps this is why the Aramaic refers to the devil as Uprightness – because Uprightness is the end result of this encounter. *When the devil had finished all this tempting, he left him until an opportune time. Then Jesus returned in the power of the Spirit (Luke 4:13-14 NIV).* Jesus returned from the devil, not defeated but empowered, upright and ready for His ministry.

THE DEVIL MADE ME DO IT

What CREDIT or BLAME does the devil deserve?

If God is the author, source and creator of ALL THINGS then everything, including Satan or the devil or (d)evil also comes from God. The adversary / serpent that "tempted" Eve to partake of the forbidden knowledge of good and evil is traditionally *blamed* for the "Fall of man." Following this same line of thinking, the adversary that Jesus is driven to "by the Spirit" to be tempted of, and then consequently returns from "with power" must then be *credited* for helping in the preparation process of Jesus' ministry.

In actuality, the role and efficacy of the (d)evil is specifically tied to human response and can be seen as either evil in one context or good in another depending on the mind of the person perceiving the experience as either a "temptation" or a "preparation." Often we, ourselves consciously create circumstances that lead toward goodness and peace; but we can also unconsciously create an environment that produces evil and violence.

Consider the next two verses that clearly tell us that God creates and sustains the existence of all things – including *dominions, rulers, and authorities*. The scripture goes so far as to explain that even the WICKED are fitted for their role and operate within the PURPOSE of God.

For it was in Him that ALL THINGS were created, in heaven and on earth, things seen and things unseen, whether thrones, dominions, rulers, or authorities; all things were created and exist through Him [by His service, intervention] and in and FOR HIM. And He Himself existed before ALL THINGS, and in Him ALL THINGS consist (cohere, are held together).
Colossians 1:16-17 - AMP

The Lord has made EVERYTHING [to accommodate itself and contribute] to its own end and HIS OWN PURPOSE; EVEN THE WICKED [are fitted for their role] for the day of calamity and EVIL.
Proverbs 16:4 – AMP

GOD OR DEVIL? G(O)OD OR (D)EVIL?

In this section an exhaustive list of passages in both the Old and New Testaments will provide us with a solid foundation for building a God-centric (not devil centered) consciousness and understanding of scripture:

See now that I, I am He, and there is no god beside Me; I KILL and I make alive, I WOUND and I heal, and there is none who can deliver out of My hand.
Deuteronomy 32:39 - AMP

And I will restore or replace for you the years that the locust has eaten-the hopping locust, the stripping locust, and the crawling locust, MY GREAT ARMY WHICH I SENT AMONG YOU.
Joel 2:25

When a trumpet sounds in a city, do not the people tremble? When disaster comes to a city, HAS NOT THE LORD CAUSED IT?
Amos 3:6 – TNIV

Notice in the next three passages that what most modern day Christians would have blamed on the devil was actually God working behind the scenes for a greater purpose of which we may not have been aware. Pay close attention to the terminology – *GOD SENT an EVIL SPIRIT* and an *EVIL SPIRIT FROM GOD!*

*And GOD SENT AN EVIL SPIRIT between Abimelech and the men
of Shechem, and the men of Shechem dealt
treacherously with Abimelech.*
Judges 9:23 - AMP

*But the Spirit of the Lord departed from Saul, and an EVIL SPIRIT
FROM THE LORD tormented and troubled him. Saul's servants
said to him, Behold, an EVIL SPIRIT FROM GOD torments you.
Let our lord now command your servants here before you to find
a man who plays skillfully on the lyre; and when the EVIL SPIRIT
FROM GOD is upon you, he will play it, and you will be well. And
when the EVIL SPIRIT FROM GOD was upon Saul, David took a
lyre and played it; so Saul was refreshed and became well,
and the evil spirit left him.*
I Samuel 16:14-16, 23 – AMP

*The next day an EVIL SPIRIT FROM GOD came mightily upon
Saul, and he raved [madly] in his house, while David played [the
lyre] with his hand, as at other times;
and there was a javelin in Saul's hand.*
I Samuel 18:10 - AMP

In this next scripture reference, God needs to redirect and even
confuse Ahab. The biblical passage seems to indicate that this
NEUTRAL spirit comes forth and says to God, "Use me how You
will in order to accomplish Your purpose. If You need me to be a
LYING SPIRIT, then that's what I'll be." God agrees to it and gives
the mission a blessing! Statements such as this are not blaming
evil on God or attributing evil to God, but rather are giving the
Universe back to God, or acknowledging the fact that control of
the Universe has been His all along. The concept that God has the
power to and often does use what we (with our finite human minds
and understanding) would consider evil for His ultimate good is

only foreign to us because we have given half the control of the Universe (in our minds) over to another entity (the devil) whom we have come to believe is as powerful as God. Do we believe that God truly works ALL things for our good as it says in Romans, or don't we?

And the Lord said, who will entice Ahab to go up and fall at Ramoth-gilead? One said this way, another said that way. Then there came forth a spirit [of whom I am about to tell] and stood before the Lord and said, I will entice him. The Lord said to him, By what means? And he said, I will go forth and be a LYING SPIRIT in the mouths of all his prophets. [The Lord] said, You shall entice him and succeed also. Go forth and do it. SO THE LORD HAS PUT A LYING SPIRIT in the mouths of all these prophets; and the Lord has spoken evil concerning you.
I Kings 22:20-23 / II Chronicles 18:18-22 – AMP

At other times in scripture, Satan is seen as an "accuser" who brings a charge against humanity before God (as in the story of Job). Yet, we must remember that in this story GOD INITIATES the conversation with the devil and then SETS THE BOUNDARIES that this *accuser* must operate within and be respectful of.

Here are two verses from the story of Job. One verse describes Job being placed IN THE HAND of Satan for a period of testing. The other verse comes at the end of the story where Job realizes that this testing was the LORD'S DOING all the while, not the devil's.

And the Lord said to SATAN, BEHOLD, HE IS IN YOUR HAND; only spare his life.
Job 2:6 - AMP

*And the Lord turned the captivity of Job and restored his fortunes,
when he prayed for his friends; also the Lord gave Job TWICE
as much as he had before.*
*Then there came to him all his brothers and sisters and all who
had known him before, and they ate bread with him in his house;
and they sympathized with him and comforted him over ALL THE
[distressing] CALAMITIES THAT THE LORD HAD BROUGHT
UPON HIM. Every man also gave him a piece of money, and every
man an earring of gold. After this, Job lived 140 years, and saw
his sons and his sons' sons, even to four generations.*
So Job died, an old man and full of days.
Job 42:10-11, 17- AMP

The good news is that because Job was able to "endure to the end"
he received double for all that he lost, and after the testing (of God,
not the devil) Job lived a full and blessed life. The question is this,
wasn't Job in the HAND OF GOD the whole time? This lesson
illustrates to us why mankind was told by God to eat of the TREE OF
LIFE and to avoid the TREE OF THE KNOWLEDGE OF GOOD
AND EVIL. Many times what seems like the devil may actually be
God working to bring us into a higher level of consciousness and
into a greater season of blessing. We may not always understand
the "behind the scenes" workings of God, but we can trust that God
desires to bless us and not curse us!

In these two passages taken from Isaiah, God is Creator of LIGHT
and DARKNESS; He Creates both WELL BEING and CALAMITY.
He also creates the BLACKSMITH...who creates the WEAPON...
which cannot prosper against us. Why is it that "No weapon formed
against us" is able to prosper? Because in reality...THERE IS NO
WEAPON, only situations that God allows to bring us higher in
purpose and in consciousness!

I am the Lord, and there is no one else; there is no God besides Me. I will gird and arm you, though you have not known Me, That men may know from the east and the rising of the sun and from the west and the setting of the sun that there is no God besides Me. I am the Lord, and no one else [is He]. I form the light and CREATE DARKNESS, I make peace [national well-being] and I CREATE [physical] EVIL (calamity); I AM THE LORD WHO DOES ALL THESE THINGS.
Isaiah 45:5-7 – AMP

Many names exist to define and describe different attributes of God. Jehovah Jireh means *God our Provider*. Jehovah Shalom means the *God of our Peace*. What if the name SATAN is merely another expression of God? If God did indeed create everything, where else could Satan, darkness, evil – whatever label we choose to give it – have come from?

Behold, I have created the smith who blows on the fire of coals and who produces a weapon for its purpose; and I have created the DEVASTATOR TO DESTROY.
But no weapon that is formed against you shall prosper, and every tongue that shall rise against you in judgment you shall show to be in the wrong. This [peace, righteousness, security, triumph over opposition] is the heritage of the servants of the Lord [those in whom the ideal Servant of the Lord is reproduced]; this is the righteousness or the vindication which they obtain from Me [this is that which I impart to them as their justification], says the Lord.
Isaiah 54:16-17 - AMP

II Samuel and I Chronicles are basically mirror books. What is referred to in II Samuel as the "anger of the Lord" is later seen in the same story in I Chronicles as "Satan." What one consciousness sees as the devil another accepts as the handiwork of God!

Again the ANGER OF THE LORD was kindled against Israel, and
He moved David against them, saying, Go,
number Israel and Judah.
II Samuel 24:1 - AMP

SATAN [an adversary] stood up against Israel and
stirred up David to number Israel.
I Chronicles 21:1 - AMP

Now let us compare these two verses. In Matthew, when Peter stands between Jesus and His destiny at Calvary, Jesus calls Peter SATAN. Then in John, when SATAN enters Judas, he is "possessed" to "betray" or lead Christ to the cross. Jesus rebukes the Satan in Peter but affirms the Satan in Judas. The differentiation seems to be that in one instance Satan is standing in the way of Christ's destiny and in the other, he is pushing or leading Christ toward His destiny.

Peter took him aside and began to rebuke him. "Never, Lord!" he
said. "This shall never happen to you!" Jesus turned and SAID
TO PETER, "GET BEHIND ME SATAN! You are a stumbling
block to me; you do not have in mind the things of God,
but the things of men."
Matthew 16:22-23 - NIV

Then after [he had taken] the bit of food, SATAN entered into and
took possession of [Judas]. Jesus said to him, What you are going
to do, do more swiftly than you seem to intend and
make quick work of it.
John 13:27 - AMP

For the creation (nature) was subjected to frailty (to futility, condemned to frustration), not because of some intentional fault on its part, BUT BY THE WILL OF HIM WHO SUBJECTED IT - [yet] with the hope that nature (creation) itself will be set free from its bondage to decay and corruption [and gain an entrance] into the glorious freedom of God's children.
Romans 8:20-21 - AMP

In the next two passages in Romans (9:15-23 and 11:28-36) we will use the previous passage from Romans 8 to serve as a foundation for our understanding: GOD, not the devil or Adam, subjected the creation to *bondage* so that He might introduce it to *freedom!* Also, pay special attention to the explanations offered to us in the parenthesis of this Amplified translation.

For He says to Moses, I will have mercy on whom I will have mercy and I will have compassion (pity) on whom I will have compassion. So then [God's gift] IS NOT A QUESTION OF HUMAN WILL AND HUMAN EFFORT, but of God's mercy. [It depends not on one's own willingness nor on his strenuous exertion as in running a race, but on God's having mercy on him.] For the Scripture says to PHARAOH, I HAVE RAISED YOU UP for this very purpose of DISPLAYING MY POWER [dealing with] YOU, so that MY NAME MAY BE PROCLAIMED THE WHOLE WORLD OVER. So then He has mercy on whomever He wills (chooses) and HE HARDENS (makes stubborn and unyielding the heart of) WHOMEVER HE WILLS. You will say to me, Why then does He still find fault and blame us [for sinning]? For who can resist and withstand His will? But who are you, a mere man, to criticize and contradict and answer back to God? Will what is formed say to him that formed it, Why have you made me thus? Has the potter no right over the clay, to make out of the same mass (lump) one vessel for beauty and distinction and honorable use, and another for menial or ignoble and dishonorable use? What if

*God, although fully intending to show [the awfulness of] His wrath
and to make known His power and authority, has tolerated with
much patience the vessels (objects) of [His] anger which are ripe
for destruction? And [what if] He thus purposes to make known
and show the wealth of His glory in [dealing with] the vessels
(objects) of His mercy which He has prepared
beforehand for glory."*
Romans 9:15-23 – AMP

*From the point of view of the Gospel (good news), they [the
Jews, at present] are enemies [of God], which is FOR YOUR
ADVANTAGE and benefit. But from the point of view of God's
choice (of election, of divine selection), THEY ARE STILL
BELOVED (dear to Him) for the sake of their forefathers. For
God's gifts and His call are irrevocable. [He never withdraws them
when once they are given, and He does not change His mind about
those to whom He gives His grace or to whom He sends His call.]*

*Just as you were once disobedient and rebellious toward God
but now have obtained [His] mercy, through their disobedience,
So they also now are being disobedient [when you are receiving
mercy], THAT THEY IN TURN MAY ONE DAY, THROUGH THE
MERCY YOU ARE ENJOYING, ALSO RECEIVE MERCY.
FOR GOD HAS CONSIGNED (penned up) ALL MEN TO
DISOBEDIENCE, ONLY THAT HE MAY HAVE MERCY ON
THEM ALL [alike]. Oh, the depth of the riches and wisdom and
knowledge of God! How unfathomable (inscrutable, unsearchable)
are His judgments (His decisions)! And how untraceable
(mysterious, undiscoverable) are His ways (His methods, His
paths)! For who has known the mind of the Lord and who has
understood His thoughts, or who has [ever] been His counselor?
Or who has first given God anything that he might be paid back
or that he could claim a recompense? FOR FROM HIM AND
THROUGH HIM AND TO HIM ARE ALL THINGS. [For all things*

originate with Him and come from Him; all things live through Him, and all things center in and tend to consummate and to end in Him.] To Him be glory forever! Amen (so be it).
Romans 11:28-36 – AMP

So much revelation is contained in these passages from Romans. Allow me to lay it out plainly so that we can take it all in:

➤ God has mercy on whomever He wants.

➤ Mercy is GOD'S GIFT (*it IS NOT A QUESTION OF HUMAN WILL AND HUMAN EFFORT, but of God's mercy...It depends not on one's own willingness nor on his strenuous exertion as in running a race, but on God's having mercy on him*).

➤ God raises up Pharaoh, displays His power in him, and then hardens his heart for HIS OWN PURPOSES.

➤ Then the Question: *Why then does He still find fault and blame us [for sinning]? For who can resist and withstand His will?* In other words, if God hardened Pharaoh's heart, how can we - or better - how can God blame Pharaoh? This seems like a tough question until we realize that without God hardening Pharaoh's heart the Israelites would never have left the bondage of Egypt to eventually realize the freedom that awaited them in the Promised Land.

➤ *Vessels of Honor* and *Dishonor* are *prepared beforehand* so that God might show mercy *ON ALL!*

➤ The Jews' disobedience was a *gift* and *calling* from God that was *irrevocable*.

> Gentiles (us, we) obtained mercy through the Jews' disobedience.

> God puts ALL MEN into disobedience that He may have MERCY ON ALL - *FOR GOD HAS CONSIGNED (penned up) ALL MEN TO DISOBEDIENCE, ONLY THAT HE MAY HAVE MERCY ON THEM ALL [alike].*

> God's ways are higher than our ways - *How unfathomable (inscrutable, unsearchable) are His judgments (His decisions)! And how untraceable (mysterious, undiscoverable) are His ways (His methods, His paths)!* So then, we must *walk by faith, and not by sight!* We must trust that God is GOOD; that God's mercy ENDURES FOREVER; and that God declares the END FROM THE BEGINNING!

> IT'S ALL GOD...and even though we may struggle to see it clearly...IT'S ALL GOOD! *FOR FROM HIM AND THROUGH HIM AND TO HIM ARE ALL THINGS. [For all things originate with Him and come from Him; all things live through Him, and all things center in and tend to consummate and to end in Him.]*

IT'S ALL GOD (dispelling Duality)

Is creation doomed to exist dualistically (at least in thought)? In other words, is the Universe divided into Good and Evil? God and Devil? Or does everything come from God, exist in God, work for God, and ultimately bring glory to God?

FOR FROM HIM AND THROUGH HIM AND TO HIM ARE ALL THINGS. [For all things originate with Him and come from Him; all things live through Him, and all things center in and tend to consummate and to end in Him.] To Him be glory forever! Amen (so be it).
Romans 11:36 - AMP

For by Him ALL THINGS were created that are in heaven and that are on earth, visible and invisible, whether thrones or dominions or principalities or powers. ALL THINGS were created THROUGH HIM and FOR HIM. And He is before all things, and IN HIM ALL THINGS CONSIST. And He is the head of the body, the church, who is the beginning, the firstborn from the dead, that in ALL THINGS He may have the preeminence.
Colossians 1:15-22 NIV

If the Garden of Eden is thought of as God's original intention and ultimate environment for man, how will we ever find our way back to this paradise if all we do is repeat, condone and even teach others to adopt the very consciousness that expelled us from the Garden? The Knowledge of GOOD and EVIL – that forbidden fruit – will only allow a strict and provincial vision of God. Dualistic consciousness will never provide us with a panoramic view of the sovereignty and providence of God. Until we perceive and accept that there is only One Power in the Universe we will never truly understand or possess true power.

Consider the next three verses where "SATAN" is used by God to:

➢ Discipline, destroy carnal lusts and to "SAVE" a person

➢ Keep Paul humble so that he may continue to receive revelation from God

➢ Teach Paul's disciples not to blaspheme

You are to DELIVER THIS MAN OVER TO SATAN for physical DISCIPLINE [to destroy carnal lusts which prompted him to incest], that [his] SPIRIT MAY [yet] BE SAVED in the day of the Lord Jesus.
I Corinthians 5:5 – AMP

And to keep me from being puffed up and too much elated by the exceeding greatness (preeminence) of these revelations, THERE WAS GIVEN ME a thorn (a splinter) in the flesh, A MESSENGER OF SATAN, to rack and buffet and harass me, to keep me from being excessively exalted. Three times I called upon the Lord and besought [Him] about this and begged that it might depart from me; But He said to me, My grace (My favor and loving-kindness and mercy) is enough for you [sufficient against any danger and enables you to bear the trouble manfully]; for My strength and power are made perfect (fulfilled and completed) and show themselves most effective in [your] weakness. Therefore, I will all the more gladly glory in my weaknesses and infirmities, that the strength and power of Christ (the Messiah) may rest (yes, may pitch a tent over and dwell) upon me!
II Corinthians 12:7-9 - AMP

Among them are Hymenaeus and Alexander, whom I HAVE DELIVERED TO SATAN in order that they may be disciplined [by punishment and learn] NOT TO BLASPHEME.
I Timothy 1:20 - AMP

Now, let's review. In these scriptures, SATAN is SAVING, HUMBLING and TEACHING mankind how to be more divine? That sounds an awful lot like the work of God.

Also, consider this most troubling, yet transformative, idea. The Apostle Paul is responsible for giving us the greater majority of what we call the New Testament Bible. According to *II Corinthians 12*, Satan is used as an agent to keep Paul humble so that he might continue to receive "revelation" from God and eventually author book after book, epistle after epistle, of divine thought from God to man. In other words, God used Satan to keep Paul in a place of consciousness so that he could give us the New Testament. So, is Satan to be credited, at least partially, with giving us a portion of the Bible? Or in the end isn't it God who gets the glory?

Notice Paul recognizes two key truths regarding this:

➢ This *thorn* or *messenger* was *GIVEN TO HIM*. Given by whom? Given by God! How do we know this messenger (of Satan) was given to Paul by God?

➢ Paul pleads for this messenger to leave on three occasions. And, three times God tells Paul "NO! I sent it and it cannot leave until it has accomplished in you what I please. But, in the midst of this seemingly trying time, I am also sending you My grace. And, it will be sufficient for you!"

NO OTHER GOD (Not even the devil)

The commonly held theological belief among many Christians and Christian denominations (that prescribe to an eternal hell that if the world ended today will claim a greater majority of human souls than heaven will) is that God is only slightly more powerful than the devil, and that the possibility exists that on a bad day God could slip up and lose creation to the devil. This *Star Wars* like thinking tends to magnify the *Dark Side* as being so powerful that the *Force* is constantly, and perhaps unconsciously, being minimized. Further, according to this theological scenario, the final outcome always seems to be in jeopardy or even left up to chance.

As we study the progression of God's truth throughout the Bible, we find a continually flowing stream of thought that is capable of watering the God consciousness within us. What is this stream carrying to us? The idea that God is all there is! Remember Christianity is a MONOTHEISTIC religion. We believe in ONE GOD, not many. No matter what names are used for God (Jehovah, Yahweh, Jireh, Shalom...Krishna, Allah, etc.) there is only God! Consider the many passages that give us the simple truth – there is no other God...but God.

To you it was shown, that you might know that the LORD Himself is God; there is NONE OTHER besides Him.
Deuteronomy 4:35 - NKJV

Therefore know this day, and consider it in your heart, that the LORD Himself is God in heaven above and on the earth beneath; there is NO OTHER.
Deuteronomy 4:39 - NKJV

*That all the peoples of the earth may know that the LORD is God;
there is NO OTHER.*
I Kings 8:60 - NKJV

*Thus says the LORD, the King of Israel, And his Redeemer, the
LORD of hosts: ' I am the First and I am the Last; BESIDES ME
THERE IS NO GOD. And who can proclaim as I do? Do not fear,
nor be afraid; Have I not told you from that time, and declared it?
You are My witnesses. IS THERE A GOD BESIDES ME? INDEED
THERE IS NO OTHER ROCK; I KNOW NOT ONE.*
Isaiah 44:6-8 - NKJV

The *45th Chapter of Isaiah* is full of this declaration that God is all
there is. Pay close attention to the ideas here that reveal God creates
Light and Darkness – Peace and Calamity; not the devil. Many
skeptics would attempt to write off some of these verses as solely
dealing with idol worship. However, we find here that God is not
only saying that idol worship is a waste of time – since all there is…
is God. But, this specific passage in Isaiah reveals that there is NO
OTHER GOD…not even the devil!

*v. 5 I am the LORD, and THERE IS NO OTHER; There is NO GOD
BESIDES ME.*

*v. 6-7 That they may know from the rising of the sun to its setting,
That THERE IS NONE BESIDES ME. I am the LORD, and THERE
IS NO OTHER; I form the light and create darkness, I make peace
and create calamity; I, the LORD, do all these things.*

*v. 14 Surely God is in you, And THERE IS NOT OTHER; THERE IS
NO OTHER GOD.*

v. 18 I am the LORD, and THERE IS NO OTHER.

v. 21 And THERE IS NO OTHER GOD BESIDES ME, A just God and a Savior;

v. 22 For I am God, and THERE IS NO OTHER.

In the *46th Chapter* of Isaiah we see that there is no force EQUAL in power to God in the universe; none to be COMPARED to God. The way we have MAGNIFIED the devil and the power of hell, while MINIMIZING God and the power of the cross must be reconsidered.

To whom will you liken Me, and MAKE ME EQUAL, And COMPARE ME, that we should be alike? Remember the former things of old, For I am God, and THERE IS NO OTHER; I am God, and THERE IS NONE LIKE ME
Isaiah 46:5, 9 - NKJV

I am the LORD your God, And there is NO OTHER. My people shall never be put to shame.
Joel 2:27 - NKJV

Then one of the scribes came, and having heard them reasoning together, perceiving that He had answered them well, asked Him, "Which is the first commandment of all?" Jesus answered him, "The first of all the commandments is: 'Hear, O Israel, the LORD our God, the LORD IS ONE. And you shall love the LORD your God with all your heart, with all your soul, with all your mind, and with all your strength.' This is the first commandment. And the second, like it, is this: 'You shall love your neighbor as yourself.' There is no other commandment greater than these." So the scribe said to Him, "Well said, Teacher. You have spoken the truth, for THERE IS ONE GOD, AND THERE IS NO OTHER BUT HE. And to love Him with all the heart, with all the understanding, with all

the soul, and with all the strength, and to love one's neighbor as
oneself, is more than all the whole burnt offerings and sacrifices."
Now when Jesus saw that he answered wisely, He said to him,
"YOU ARE NOT FAR FROM THE KINGDOM OF GOD."
But after that no one dared question Him.
Mark 12:28-34 - NKJV

We are not FAR FROM THE KINGDOM as we realize that GOD IS
ONE – that there is only ONE GOD.

Therefore concerning the eating of things offered to idols,
we know that an idol is nothing in the world, and that
THERE IS NO OTHER GOD BUT ONE.
I Corinthians 8:4 - NKJV

The Message Bible goes as far as to say that idols (and other gods)
don't even exist. This doesn't mean that other cultures and peoples
are worshipping something that doesn't exist. It simply means that
no matter how many names are ascribed to God – all there is…is
God. Yet, people in various cultures and religions connect to the
same God in a diversity of ways.

Some people say, quite rightly, that IDOLS HAVE NO ACTUAL
EXISTENCE, that there's nothing to them, that THERE IS NO
GOD other than our ONE GOD, that no matter how many of these
so-called gods are named and worshiped they still don't add up to
anything but a tall story. They say—again, quite rightly—that there
is only ONE GOD the Father, that everything comes from him.
I Corinthians 8:4-6 Message Bible

Consider the truths of the ONE GOD ideal that we can glean from Paul's interaction with, and message to, the philosophers at Athens:

for as I was passing through and considering the objects of your worship, I even found an altar with this inscription: TO THE UNKNOWN GOD. Therefore, the One whom you worship without knowing, Him I proclaim to you
Acts 17:23 - NKJV

Paul is clearly saying to the philosophers "what you call *the UNKNOWN GOD* I may call another name. However, there is only God." That's why Paul says to them that the God you are already worshipping – *"HIM I PROCLAIM TO YOU."* Not another God - the one you are already worshipping! Paul gives further clarity to this idea of ONE GOD by declaring to these Athenian philosophers...

...in Him WE live and move and have OUR being, as also some of your own poets have said, 'For WE are also His offspring.' Therefore, since WE are the offspring of God...
Acts 17:28-29 - NKJV

In other words, Paul tells them, you are already *living* and *moving* and having your *being in Him* - THE ONE GOD – even if you are not aware of it yet. This is why Paul continues throughout his sermon to use inclusive language – *WE* live, *WE* move, *WE* have *OUR* being in Him.

Paul then agrees with their philosophy that ALL MEN are the offspring of God thus Paul responds, *since WE are the offspring of God.*

IF GOD IS ALL THERE IS...

Question: If God is all there is, then why is there hunger in the world?

Answer: There is enough food in the world so that no human should ever have to die of starvation. In America alone, we throw away more than one-third the food that we produce.

Question: If God is all there is, then why are people dying of disease?

Answer: There is enough medicine in the world that if distributed appropriately, could ensure that no one ever die needlessly from simple diseases and sicknesses like malaria, measles, chicken pox, typhoid, polio, diarrhea, dehydration, etc.

Question: If God is all there is, then why does war continue?

Answer: Humanity has the power to end war anytime it wants.

The simple answer is that we are created in the *IMAGE and LIKENESS of God (Genesis 1:26)*. Therefore, we innately have the power to create our reality. And, when we choose to do so, we also possess the power to recreate our reality when we grow tired of the old reality.

The reason God does not "fix" the world is because God has given us the power to do it. If God has the power to fix the world, but will not do it, what does this say of God? Is God malicious? Absentee? Neglectful? Oblivious? It would seem so. However, when we realize that WE have the power to do what we are asking God to do then God is no longer viewed as torturing us, all of the sudden, God is seen as teaching us!

We must wake up to the truth that we carry divinity within humanity – much like Jesus did (our *elder brother* and the *firstborn among MANY brethren*). The psalmist goes so far as to say that we are "gods." Then later, Jesus repeats this idea to the Pharisees and even reinforces this idea by quoting their scriptures back to them.

> *I have said, YE ARE GODS; and all of you are*
> *children of the most High.*
> **Psalm 82:6 - KJV**

> *I and my Father are one. Then the Jews took up stones again to stone him.*
> *Jesus answered them, Many good works have I shewed you from my Father; for which of those works do ye stone me? The Jews answered him, saying, For a good work we stone thee not; but for blasphemy; and because that thou, being a man, makest thyself God. Jesus answered them, Is it not written in YOUR LAW, I said, 'YE ARE GODS?'*
> **John 10:30-34 - KJV**

As we accept our god-likeness (and only when we accept our god-likeness), we will begin to take responsibility for what we create and have created, and we will cease to blame God for things that God is not responsible for. This acceptance, however, is very difficult for a mind that has been conditioned to believe that we are separate from and innately different from God. Realizing this war that often takes place in the religious mind Jesus even attempts to point out to the Pharisees that this idea didn't originate with Him, but with THEIR LAW!

David initially struggles to accept this awesome wonderment of being made in the likeness of divinity but finally recognizes that man is more than just innately sinful; or evil; or even *other* than God.

> *Surely I was sinful at birth, sinful from the time*
> *my mother conceived me.*
> **Psalm 51:5 - NIV**

> *I praise you because I am fearfully and wonderfully made;*
> *your works are wonderful, I know that full well.*
> **Psalm 139:14 - NIV**

Also, be aware that the Pharisees fought this idea so vehemently that they were ready to stone Jesus for surrendering to and then claiming His own divinity (as seen in the aforementioned passage *John 10:30-34 KJV*). Yet, Jesus, in essence, says to them, "Not only am I God, but you all are also gods!"

On another occasion, Jesus informs the Pharisees that the Kingdom of God is within them even if they do not realize it! The same Pharisees that Jesus called – "Brood of vipers," "empty tombs," and "sons of the devil" He also declares to be "gods" and carriers of the "kingdom." We have the same potential to become at one with our divinity as Jesus did. The choice is ours as to which nature we will feed and foster. Humanity? Iniquity? Sinfulness? Fallenness? Or Divinity?

> *Once, having been asked by the Pharisees when the kingdom of*
> *God would come, Jesus replied, "The kingdom of God does not*
> *come with your careful observation, nor will people say, 'Here it*
> *is,' or 'There it is,' because the kingdom of God is within you."*
> **Luke 17:20-21 - NIV**

The way we know Jesus was referring to the Pharisees here is because it was the Pharisees who were asking Him the question *(Once, having been asked by the Pharisees when the kingdom of God would come).* So, Jesus' answer was to the Pharisees. And, what was His answer? That the Kingdom of God is within the Pharisees!

Paul seemed to vacillate between opinions regarding man's divinity and innate sinfulness. In these next two passages, Paul refers to himself as a sinful and *wretched man* - and then proclaims that we are *being transformed into the image of God's glory* and will one day look into the *mirror* and see this glory in our own reflection! This would seem to reinforce the idea that in this earthly realm we are imperfectly walking into our Christ-like perfection.

I do not understand what I do. For what I want to do I do not do, but what I hate I do. I know that nothing good lives in me, that is, in my sinful nature. For I have the desire to do what is good, but I cannot carry it out. For what I do is not the good I want to do; no, the evil I do not want to do—this I keep on doing. So I find this law at work: When I want to do good, evil is right there with me. What a wretched man I am! Who will rescue me from this body of death? Thanks be to God—through Jesus Christ our Lord!
Romans 7:15, 18-19, 21, 24-25 NIV

Nevertheless when one turns to the Lord, the veil is taken away. Now the Lord is the Spirit; and where the Spirit of the Lord is, there is liberty. But we all, with unveiled face, BEHOLDING AS IN A MIRROR THE GLORY OF THE LORD, are being transformed into the same image from glory to glory, just as by the Spirit of the Lord.
II Corinthians 3:16-18 NKJV

How do we transition from being a sinful humanity into being spiritual divinity? We follow the example of our *elder brother*. We follow the pattern of Jesus the Christ; the *firstborn among many brethren!*

> ➤ If God is all there is...then we must repent (or rethink) our view of the Universe.

> ➤ If God is all there is...then we are not separate from or different from God.

> ➤ If God is all there is...then it's ALL GOOD, because it's ALL GOD!

> ➤ If God is all there is...then we must refuse to compare or equate any supposed devil, or any perceived evil, with God!

HOW TO DEAL WITH THE DEVIL

➤ Make NO PLACE for the (d)evil! (Ephesians 4:27 - NKJV). One way in which we make no place for the devil is by refusing to allow our Spiritual life and thought-life to become "devil-centric." We must consciously decide to remove the devil from our minds and mouths (that is IF we want the devil out of our lives)!

➤ RESIST THE DEVIL (by submitting to God) and he will flee (James 4:7 – NKJV)! One way in which we resist the devil is by not blaming the devil for circumstances that we create ourselves - or by crediting the devil through misinterpreting tests (or texts) that God sends to prepare us for greater revelation, growth and power.

➤ Remember that ALL THINGS were CREATED BY GOD – ALL THINGS EXIST FOR GOD – and ALL THINGS are HELD TOGETHER IN GOD...including the devil! (Colossians 1:16-17 – AMP)

➤ God sets before us "LIFE and Death...BLESSING and Cursing."

This day I call heaven and earth as witnesses against you that I have set before you life and death, blessings and curses. NOW CHOOSE LIFE, so that you and your children may live and that you may love the LORD your God, listen to his voice, and hold fast to him. For the LORD is your life, and he will give you many years in the land he swore to give to your fathers, Abraham, Isaac and Jacob.
Deuteronomy 30:19-20 - NIV

So choose wisely. The wise choice is the TREE of LIFE (not the TREE of the KNOWLEDGE of GOOD and EVIL - or the duality of God and Devil).

> ➢ Remember to Rejoice…It's ALL GOOD because It's ALL GOD!

Worthy are You, our Lord and God, to receive the glory and the honor and dominion, FOR YOU CREATED ALL THINGS; BY YOUR WILL THEY WERE [brought into being] AND WERE CREATED.
Revelation 4:11 – AMP

The Holy Bible of Inclusion

Part IV - THE PURPOSE OF HELL ... AND THE FIRE OF GOD

---◆---

-Hell's Coming With Me –
✳

-Concentrated Statement on HELL and the FIRE of GOD-
✳

-Four words used for HELL in the 1600's-
✳

-ETERNAL PUNISHMENT-
✳

-Sheol / Hades-
✳

-Gehenna-
✳

-The FIRE of GOD-
✳

-ETERNAL FIRE (or AGE-DURING)?-
✳

-AFTER THE FIRE-
✳

HELL'S COMING WITH ME

I don't know about anyone else, but I often feel God speaks to me through movies. One of my favorites is *Tombstone*, the story of heroic U.S. Marshal, Wyatt Earp. In the days when the American West was still being settled it was referred to as the Wild West due to its distinct lack of established law and order.

In the following scene from the movie, Wyatt and several of his companions, who had all been duly deputized, find themselves in a stand-off with a group of renegade lawbreakers known as the Cowboys. This is the same group of men who have recently killed one of Wyatt Earp's brothers and shot and wounded another. Gunfire erupts and the members of the two opposing parties run for cover. The camera cuts to Wyatt's face, on which is an obvious expression of righteous indignation. He begins to say to himself, "No . . . no . . . no" each "no" in succession growing louder and containing more conviction than the last.

At length he stands and emerges from behind the fallen log that has served as his protection, wades fearlessly into the river, shotgun aimed in the general direction of the Cowboys, defiantly daring any or all of them to come and meet him. His brave act succeeds in drawing out the group's leader whom he shoots and kills as well as several others who have foolishly followed. In the very next scene, the men with Earp, including his friend, Doc Holliday are discussing what has just transpired.

Man #1: "Did you ever see anything like that before?"

Man #2: "Hell, I ain't never heard of anything like that."

Man #1: "Where is he?"

Doc: "Down by the creek, walking on water."

Man #1: "Well, let's hope he's got another miracle up his sleeve, 'cause if I know Ringo, he's headed straight for us. If they were my brothers, I'd want revenge too."

Doc: "Oh, make no mistake. It's not revenge he's after. It's a reckoning."

Something about that scene resonates with every human being, myself included. We have within us a deep desire for justice; for wrongs to be made right; for those who commit evil acts (especially against those we love or people we perceive as innocent victims) to pay for their crimes.

This is a very normal human emotional response. However, notice that Doc Holliday makes a distinction between revenge (to exact punishment for a wrong, especially in a resentful or vindictive spirit) and what he refers to as a reckoning (an accounting for things received or done). This is a subtle but important difference, which lies totally within the heart and motive of an individual.

The Bible commands us to love our enemies, even those who despitefully use us; to turn the other cheek if someone strikes us, and not to judge others. Yet that same Bible records the story of Jesus forcefully and physically throwing the money changers out of the temple and making statements such as *those who bear the sword do not bear it in vain.* There are also numerous references in the New Testament about the power to judge belonging to the elders of the church. This is but another example of biblical contradiction.

It is completely understandable in today's present climate of rampant acts of violence (many times against innocent people for seemingly no justifiable reason) that we, as humans, need to believe that the perpetrators of these violent acts will be brought to justice and required to give an accounting and pay for what they have done.

Throughout history humankind has and continues to take upon itself the responsibility for the punishment of those who break the human laws we have set in place. Many would argue that this is the only practical and reasonable way for a civilized society to exist. And, I have no argument with that. But what we must understand is that crime and the subsequent punishment for human, earthly offenses are limited to and remain in this earthly, human realm of existence.

The need we have to see people pay for their transgressions is a direct result of our decision to eat from the Tree of the Knowledge of Good and Evil. At that point, humans took it upon themselves to judge between right and wrong. Another scene from the movie *Tombstone* perfectly illustrates exactly what we do when we decide to take on this responsibility.

Wyatt: (to Ike Clanton, who he is holding on the ground at gunpoint) "Alright, Clanton. You called down the thunder - well, you got it... You tell 'em I'm coming. And hell's coming with me, you hear? HELL'S COMING WITH ME!"

More than any physical realm where unrepentant sinners are sent, hell is a consciousness. Just as Wyatt Earp declared here, we, as humans, indeed have the ability to "bring hell with us" and we often do when we, through means of both revenge and reckoning, mete out punishment to our fellow man. In order to maintain an orderly society, this is completely justifiable and even necessary at times. But what we must remember is that God is not subject to our earthly, human laws. His nature is redemptive. His laws are of a higher consciousness and thus we err when we try to compare our human ideas of justice to His.

We must also remember that when and if we choose to bring hell with us to someone else, because of the interconnected nature of humanity, we are also bringing it to ourselves. The only way of escape from this is to rise above it to a higher consciousness.

CONCENTRATED STATEMENT ON HELL AND THE FIRE OF GOD

GOD, Who is REDEMPTIVE by nature, created the earth out of His REDEMPTIVE PURPOSE *(Genesis 1:1 NKJV – In the beginning God created... bara* in Hebrew – to carve out or reshape*)*, **and in due time** *(Galatians 4:4-5 NIV – But when the TIME had FULLY COME, God sent His Son, born of a woman, born under the law, to redeem those under the law, that we might receive the full right of sons)* **sent Jesus to show us the eternal Christ because of His REDEMPTIVE PURPOSE, and reclaimed the souls of mankind** *(II Corinthians 5:18-19 KJV - And all things are of God, who hath reconciled us to himself by Jesus Christ, and hath given to us the ministry of reconciliation; To wit, that God was in Christ, reconciling the world unto himself, not imputing their trespasses unto them; and hath committed unto us the word of reconciliation)* **because of His REDEMPTIVE PURPOSE. Therefore, it is not in the nature of a REDEMPTIVE, RESTORATIVE GOD to torture eternally, or even punish temporarily, without having as the ultimate goal, REDEMPTION. As our divine parent, God teaches, corrects, disciplines and even purges the creation by fire, but never tortures without REDEMPTIVE PURPOSE. Thus, hell, and any fire associated with hell, must serve a REDEMPTIVE PURPOSE.**

As we take an in-depth look at the concept of *hell* from a scriptural perspective, we must also be courageous enough to ask, and willing to consider, some very obvious and sensible questions. Questions such as:

> ➤ Does the commonly held Christian idea of hell bring honor to God? Or disgrace?

➤ Is God a divine parent who is incapable of teaching His creation?

➤ Is God a failure?

➤ Is God a teacher or torturer?

➤ Is God punitive or purgative?

➤ Does God repeatedly instruct us to forgive our enemies while burning His eternally?

➤ If God is purposeful and the nature of God is redemptive, what redemptive purpose would eternal torture serve?

➤ If Jesus conquered and has the keys of death, hell and the grave...has He somehow, or somewhere, lost them?

➤ If we believe Satan is defeated, how can we also believe he will ultimately, and eternally, claim a higher percentage, or a greater majority, of humanity than God will?

FOUR DIFFERENT WORDS USED AS "HELL" IN THE 1600's:

Later in this section we will shine a light on how certain words were misrepresented and even changed as the Bible was being translated from Hebrew and Greek into Latin, German and eventually into English (from 1604-1611 the Church of England, first under the reign of Henry VIII and finally under the reign of King James, commissioned a translation of the English Bible).

Sheol – (Hebrew) – equivalent to Greek word Hades which means "the unseen world of the dead"… "the grave"… "death"… the GOOD and BAD alike are found here.

Hades – (Greek) – equivalent to Hebrew word *Sheol* which means "place or state of departed souls"… "the grave"… "death."

Gehenna – (Greek) – A LITERAL VALLEY near Jerusalem named for its owner, the son of Hinnom. At one time, *Gehenna* was used as a place of worship for the idol god Molech. Later, *Gehenna* was turned into the city dump by King Josiah. Animal carcasses and dismembered human body parts were thrown there and burned as refuse.

Tartaroo – (Greek) – a verb which means "to cast into Tartarus," a place of punishment for fallen angels.

These four words are all associated with and translated as *hell* in the Bible. Yet, three of these four words have very different definitions (and none of them are defined as an eternal place of torture for sinners or unbelievers). It is very common in both the Hebrew and Greek languages to have multiple meanings, and even more tenses and moods, for the same word. For example, there are four different meanings for the Hebrew equivalent of *LOVE* in scripture:

Agape – which is a godly love.

Eros – is a physical and romantic love.

Phileo – is the love of a friend.

Storge – describes a family type love.

It's ALL LOVE…yet it's ALL VERY DIFFERENT. As we research the scriptures and the translator's usage of the word hell, keep in mind that the word may be used differently in different places.

ETERNAL PUNISHMENT

God, in spelling out the consequences for Adam and Eve's sin, does not mention anything about *hell*. Their punishment was physical death, difficulty in child labor, toiling to tend the ground and a mental separation (or the illusion of separation) from God caused by sin. Further, in pronouncing punishment on Cain for murdering Abel, nothing is mentioned to him about *going to hell*. However, there were consequences IN THEIR LIFETIME for disobedience. Moses, in giving the law, has no concept of hell and never mentions it once. Yet, people were stoned or punished IN THEIR LIFETIME for disobedience.

Endless torment after death is not a consideration in the Torah. The prophets prophesy many tough consequences upon Israel for their disobedience, but eternal punishment in hell is never described. And in the New Testament, the Apostle Paul never alludes to a place of eternal punishment for the wicked or the *unsaved*.

When we consider the scenario of a literal, eternal hell with actual fire we must ask a few questions:

> ➤ If there is a physical hell with real flames – what bodies are being burned?

> ➤ When we die our bodies decay and return to dust. Are those doomed to hell given another physical body specifically for the purpose of burning it?

> ➤ And, if hell and the burning in hell are to be eternal, are these bodies in hell somehow customized bodies designed by God so that they can feel the pain of burning but never actually burn completely (as this burning must continue for eternity)?

➤ Physical bodies burning in hell? Yet, somehow eternal superhuman bodies that never entirely burn although they feel like they are burning?

What type of sadistic entity would come up with this? Leo Tolstoy, the renowned Christian thinker who is remembered for his writings that remained suppressed for years under the Communist rule in Russia, offered these ideas in his *Calendar of Wisdom* on the ignorance and impotence of punishment:

Punishment is a notion that humankind gradually outgrows. A person has done evil, so another person, or a group of people, in order to fight this evil, cannot think of anything better than to create another evil, which they call punishment. Every punishment is based, not on logic or on the feeling of justice, but on the desire to wish evil on those who have done evil to you or to another person. Capital punishment is a very clear proof that our society's organization is far from being a Christian one. Everything about our present system of punishments and about all criminal law will be thought of by future generations in the same way that we think of cannibalism or human sacrifice to ancient pagan gods. "How did they not see the uselessness and cruelty of those things which they did?" our descendents will say about us.

To punish others is like putting more wood on the fire. Every crime already has punishment in itself, and it is more cruel and more just than the punishment created by people. We should remember that the desire to punish is part of a very low animal feeling which should be suppressed, and which should not be a part of our reality.

In this particular writing, Tolstoy is merely reflecting upon and uncovering a very clear pattern of thinking supported and promoted by Jesus the Christ (specifically found in the most famous sermon given in history – *The Sermon on the Mount* – also known as *the Beatitudes*).

Ye have heard that it hath been said, An eye for an eye,
and a tooth for a tooth:
But I say unto you, That ye resist not evil: but whosoever shall
smite thee on thy right cheek, turn to him the other also. Ye have
heard that it hath been said, Thou shalt love thy neighbour, and
hate thine enemy. But I say unto you, Love your enemies, bless
them that curse you, do good to them that hate you, and pray for
them which despitefully use you, and persecute you; That ye may
be the children of your Father which is in heaven: for he maketh
his sun to rise on the evil and on the good, and sendeth rain on the
just and on the unjust. For if ye love them which love you, what
reward have ye? do not even the publicans the same? And if ye
salute your brethren only, what do ye more than others?
do not even the publicans so?
Be ye therefore perfect, even as your Father
which is in heaven is perfect.
Matthew 5:38-39, 43-48 KJV

As we consider the idea of Eternal Punishment (versus a temporary purging) allow me to point out a few truths from the Sermon on the Mount:

1) Returning evil for evil (revenge, punishment, retribution, etc.) never works and is rejected by Jesus.

-Jesus challenges the old idea of *an eye for an eye and a tooth for a tooth*. Almost two millennia after the earthly life of Jesus, Mahatma Gandhi said, *An eye for an eye eventually makes the whole world blind.*

2) We are instructed to *love our enemies, bless those who curse us, do good to those who hate us, pray for those who use us...* Why? So that *we may be called children of our Father who is in heaven.*

-Simple question here: If God is full of revenge and is seeking to punish His enemies, then wouldn't Jesus instruct us to do the same (return evil for evil) in order to be called the children of God? If our Father in heaven asks us to follow the behavioral pattern of loving enemies and blessing those who hate us, but does not follow this pattern Himself then there would be no reason for us to be called His children when we exhibit forgiveness and mercy. As we exhibit mercy we are acting just like our Father who is merciful!

3) If evil is overcome by good...then how can eternal punishment defeat evil?

-Is evil dispelled by evil? Or does Ultimate Reconciliation defeat evil? *(*Matthew 12: 22-26 NIV - *Then one was brought to Him who was demon-possessed, blind and mute; and He healed him, so that the blind and mute man both spoke and saw. And all the multitudes were amazed and said, "Could this be the Son of David?" Now when the Pharisees heard it they said, "This fellow does not cast out demons except by Beelzebub, the ruler of the demons." But Jesus knew their thoughts, and said to them: "Every kingdom divided against itself is brought to desolation, and every city or house divided against itself will not stand. If Satan casts out Satan, he is divided against himself. How then will his kingdom stand?)* Remember, no problem is solved by the same consciousness that created it. Does Jesus ask us to forgive our enemies, all the while knowing that God does not forgive His?

4) Our Father in heaven is perfect.

-Perfect in love and mercy and even in His disciplining of Creation. Perfect love does not look past injustice. Perfect love teaches a higher way and even administers tough love when necessary. But, perfect love will not torture or punish eternally (as there is nothing perfect about succumbing to the lower mind of retribution, retaliation and revenge). Perfect love is redemptive, not retaliatory. So, let us be perfect as God is perfect!

SHEOL / HADES

The Hebrew word that was translated *hell* by 54 men authorized by James, the King of England in the 17th century is *sheol* - a word with the root meaning "unseen." These men opted to translate the word *sheol* as the word hell exactly the same number of times that they translated it *the grave* (31 times each). Sheol is used as *the pit* 3 times. Yet, in the Old Testament, *sheol* was not necessarily a place of punishment, for Jacob was there (Genesis 37:35; 42:38; 44:29, 31), Job longed for it (Job 14:13), David spoke of going there (Psalm 49:15), and Jesus went there (Psalm 16:10; Acts 2:24-31). In each of these cases, these men were *unseen* because they were dead, not because they were in a place of torture.

The word *sheol* is used many times in the Old Testament to refer to national judgments, specifically in the vanishing of a nation. In Isaiah 14:13 Babylon vanished in *sheol*; in Ezekiel 26:19-21 Tyre vanished in *sheol*. In other words, these cities dried up and died. Likewise, in the New Testament, Jesus declared that Capernaum would also disappear (Matthew 11:23; 12:41; Luke 10:15; 11:29-32). These nations didn't go to a particular place, but it was prophesied that they would disappear – and they did – they completely disintegrated.

Hades is the New Testament equivalent of *sheol* and is used 11 times. In Greek mythology, *Hades* was the god of the underworld and was also used as the actual name of the underworld itself. This ancient pagan myth contained all of the elements that later carried over into Roman Catholic medieval afterlife theories (in pagan mythology there was the pleasant *Elyusium*, the miserable *Tartarus* and even the *Plains of Asphodel* where the dead wandered about in *limbo*, or between *Elyusium* and *Tartarus*. Notice the eerie similarities of these pagan afterlife ideas to the commonly held modern Catholic and Christian ideas of *Heaven, Hell* and even *Purgatory*).

KJV translates *Hades* as *hell* but the correct translation is *unseen* or *grave*. *Hades* is not exclusively pictured as a place of punishment, for the righteous man Lazarus was there (Luke 16). Jesus is also pictured there (Acts 2:27 KJV – *Because thou wilt not leave my soul in hell, neither wilt thou suffer thine Holy One to see corruption*). And in I Corinthians 15:55 Paul uses *Hades* to mean *death* (i.e. – *death / hades where is your sting?*).

The biblical concepts of hell are not original to the Hebrew writers, but rather are a conglomeration of paganism, Egyptian lore, Greek Mythology and other cultural influences. The word *Hades* came into biblical usage when the Septuagint (Greek translation of the Hebrew Bible) translators chose *Hades* to represent the Hebrew *sheol*, an Old Testament concept very different from the pagan Greek notion. *Sheol* received the dead, but there is no Old Testament account of *sheol* involving punishment.

Aside from all of this information including mistranslations, misusages and influences from other ancient lore and mythology, we must remember one very important point. Jesus possesses and controls the *keys of death and hades* - Revelation 1:18 (NKJV)

GEHENNA

Gehenna, the word that is translated *hell* in the New Testament (more accurately the Gospels), is rooted in an actual Old Testament geographical location. *Gehenna* is derived from a valley near Jerusalem that belonged to a man named *Hinnom*. Scholars say the word is a transliteration of the *Valley of the sons of Hinnom*, a valley with a violent history in the Old Testament. *Gehenna* is a literal place that the New Testament uses to describe the pain associated with the reaping of consequences caused by poor decisions, greed and an overall lack of connection to conscience regarding humanity. The references to *Hinnom (Gehenna)* in scripture deal mainly with the tragedies that would befall the Jews if they did not heed the warnings of the prophets. And these tragedies happened within several years of these prophecies (Jeremiah 7:32).

The word *Gehenna* is used twelve times in the New Testament (11 by Jesus, 1 by James). Jesus uses *Gehenna* to describe the consequences of wrong thinking. Those who were destined for *Gehenna* range from the person who lusts and refuses to gouge out his eyes to avoid temptation (Matthew 5:29-30) to anyone says *raca* or calls someone a fool (Matthew 5:21-22).

In the Sermon on the Mount (Matthew 5), Jesus speaks several times of the consequences of not controlling sinful lusts. Here Jesus uses the word *Gehenna* to describe where this type of thinking would lead the Jews of his day - to destruction. And, in 70 A.D. the Roman Empire invaded Jerusalem and the dead bodies of thousands and thousands of the slain Jews were then LITERALLY THROWN INTO GEHENNA. Jesus prophesied this event in His earthly lifetime, and in 70 A.D. it happened.

Similarly, in Matthew 23, Jesus speaks of the religious order of His day and their imminent destination in *Gehenna*...and it came to pass...in THEIR GENERATION. Consider these two verses:

*You snakes! You brood of vipers! How will you escape being
condemned to hell (Gehenna)?*
Matthew 23:33 - NIV

Truly I tell you, all this will come on THIS GENERATION.
Matthew 23:36 - NIV

THE FIRE OF GOD

All too often, the religious mind associates *fire* with hell, the devil and eternal torture. However, we will show in this section that *fire* is actually more often associated with God, and a redemptive purging. Consider these verses that depict God (not the devil) as a *Consuming Fire.*

To the Israelites the glory of the LORD looked like a consuming fire on top of the mountain.
Exodus 24:17 - NIV

For the LORD your God is a consuming fire.
Deuteronomy 4:24 - NIV

With the tip of the staff that was in his hand, the angel of the LORD touched the meat and the unleavened bread. Fire flared from the rock, consuming the meat and the bread.
And the angel of the LORD disappeared.
Judges 6:21 - NIV

Smoke rose from his nostrils; consuming fire came from his mouth, burning coals blazed out of it.
II Samuel 22:9; Psalm 18:8 - NIV

See, the Name of the LORD comes from afar, with burning anger and dense clouds of smoke; his lips are full of wrath, and his tongue is a consuming fire.
Isaiah 30:27 - NIV

Notice in all of these verses that the *Consuming Fire* is specifically associated with God and God's Glory (not with hell, the devil or torture). To understand the scriptures' usage of the word *fire* (and the phrase *Fire and Brimstone*) – let us research this word further.

Fire – in the Greek is PUR – which is the root word for Purify, Purification, Purge, Purging, Purgative, even Purgatory!

Brimstone – in the Greek is THEION from the root word *theos* which is translated Divine, Divinity, God-head, and Godlike!

If we combine the words *Fire and Brimstone* we can accurately say the *PURGING OF GOD* or the process of purging that uncovers humanity's godlikeness!

And anything else that can withstand fire must be put through the fire, and THEN IT WILL BE CLEAN. But it must also be purified with the water of cleansing.
Numbers 31:23 - NIV

The *consuming fire* that is expressed numerous times in the scripture as being synonymous with God (not Satan) serves a very necessary purpose! Let us consider these passages in the 12th chapter of Hebrews that speak of God's correction, chastening and purging as being an expression of His fatherly love for His children, not as eternal torture. Also, notice at the end of the chapter we find that this process of God discipling and disciplining the creation is spoken of as a *consuming fire!*

And you have forgotten that word of encouragement that addresses you as sons: "My son, do not make light of the Lord's discipline, and do not lose heart when he rebukes you, because the Lord disciplines those he loves, and he punishes everyone he

accepts as a son." Endure hardship as discipline; God is treating you as sons. For what son is not disciplined by his father? If you are not disciplined (and everyone undergoes discipline), then you are illegitimate children and not true sons. Moreover, we have all had human fathers who disciplined us and we respected them for it. How much more should we submit to the Father of our spirits and live! Our fathers disciplined us for a little while as they thought best; but God disciplines us for our good, that we may share in his holiness. No discipline seems pleasant at the time, but painful. LATER ON, however, it produces a harvest of righteousness and peace for those who have been trained by it.
Hebrews 12:5-11 - NIV

Therefore, since we are receiving a kingdom that cannot be shaken, let us be thankful, and so worship God acceptably with reverence and awe, for our 'God is a CONSUMING FIRE.'
Hebrews 12:28-29 - NIV

The *consuming fire* of God in this passage is not to be seen as God torturing or punishing His children, but as God teaching and purging His children. Notice the context of the entire 12th chapter of Hebrews:

In verse 2 we are told to *Look to Jesus, the AUTHOR and FINISHER of our faith!* Jesus, *began a good work in us* and will see it to *the day of perfection.*

In verse 18 we find that we have *NOT COME to a mountain (Sinai) that can be touched and that is burning with fire; to DARKNESS, GLOOM and STORM.* The mind that has not been renewed by the Holy Spirit remains stuck at Mt. Sinai, a place of *darkness, gloom and storm.* Yet, we have come to a different mountain; a place of *Good News.*

In verses 22 – 24 we discover that we *have come to MOUNT ZION, to the heavenly Jerusalem, the city of the living God. You have come to thousands upon thousands of angels in joyful assembly, to the church of the firstborn, whose names are written in heaven. You have come to God, the JUDGE OF ALL MEN, to the spirits of RIGHTEOUS MEN MADE PERFECT, to Jesus the mediator of a NEW COVENANT, and to the sprinkled blood that speaks a BETTER WORD than the blood of Abel.* The *better word* that we must hear is that the Fire of God does *not come to destroy men's live…but to save men's lives!*

John the Baptist understood the (Pur)gative and (Pur)ifying FIRE that Jesus would bring with Him.

I baptize you with water for repentance. But after me will come one who is more powerful than I, whose sandals I am not fit to carry. He will baptize you with the Holy Spirit and with fire. His winnowing fork is in his hand, and he will clear his threshing floor, gathering his wheat into the barn and burning up the chaff with unquenchable fire.
Matthew 3:11-12 - NIV

Notice in this verse from the 3rd Chapter of Matthew that the wheat is gathered into the barn, but the chaff is burned in the fire. Remember that the chaff is not separate from the wheat, but is connected to and literally a part of the wheat. The chaff is what hides and even protects the wheat; it is the covering, skin or outer layer of the wheat. So, the *fire* of God burns anything in us that hides our God, good, divine nature and likeness! Our *earthen vessel*, the *man of flesh*, will and must be burned and totally consumed by the fire of God so that the Christ in us might be revealed!

When we *rightly divide* the scripture we find the Holy Spirit acting as a purifying agent throughout the Old and New Testaments! The scripture even refers to this work of the Holy Spirit in various ways: *Tongues of FIRE – Baptism of FIRE – FIRE of the Holy Spirit.* In order for us to magnify God, we must be able to see in all of these descriptions of the Holy Spirit a (PUR)GATIVE or (PUR)IFYING WORK and not a PUNITIVE or PUNISHING WORK!

Isaiah experienced this purging of the Holy Spirit long before the Day of Pentecost in the 2nd chapter of Acts. When Isaiah is called by God to be a prophet he answers that he is a man of *unclean lips* so an angel takes a *burning coal* of fire off of the *altar of God* (not from hell) and touches it to Isaiah's lips for the (PUR)pose of (PUR)ging, not torturing or punishing.

Then I said, "It's all over! I am doomed, for I am a sinful man.
I have filthy lips, and I live among a people with filthy lips. Yet I
have seen the King, the Lord of Heaven's Armies." Then one of
the seraphim flew to me with a burning coal he had taken from
the altar with a pair of tongs. He touched my lips with it and said,
"See, this coal has touched your lips. Now your guilt is removed,
and your sins are forgiven."
Isaiah 6:5-7 - NLT

The Lord will WASH AWAY the filth of the women of Zion; he will
cleanse the bloodstains from Jerusalem by a spirit of judgment
and a SPIRIT OF FIRE.
Isaiah 4:4 - NIV

The fire Isaiah prophesied about was a *washing* and a *cleansing* fire, not one of eternal torment or punishment.

Similarly, the three Hebrew children found themselves in the fiery furnace. But a *fourth man*, the Son of God, was in the fire with them! This fire did not harm them – it actually set them free! The only thing the fire destroyed was the ropes that bound them! And, they walked out of the fire – *LOOSED and FREE* – without even the *smell of smoke on their clothes*!

Then King Nebuchadnezzar was astonished; and he rose in haste and spoke, saying to his counselors, "Did we not cast three men bound into the midst of the fire?"
They answered and said to the king, "True, O king." "Look!" he answered, "I see four men loose, walking in the midst of the fire; and they are not hurt, and the form of the fourth is like the Son of God."
Daniel 3:24-25 - NKJV

One point of importance here - the *fire* (associated with the enemy of God and seen as villainous to the Hebrews) was *seven times hotter* than usual. The number seven in scripture always represents completion and perfection. Instead of being destroyed by the fire, the Hebrew children are loosed, freed, completed and perfected by the fire! Why? Because this was the fire of God (not of hell or the devil).

Then Nebuchadnezzar was furious with Shadrach, Meshach and Abednego, and his attitude toward them changed. He ordered the furnace heated SEVEN TIMES HOTTER than usual.
Daniel 3:19 - NKJV

We find further evidence that God is involved with using fire to purge creation when we discover that the *Son of God* was in the fire with the three Hebrew children!

ETERNAL FIRE (OR AGE-DURING)?

44 times we find ETERNAL LIFE in the Bible.

4 times we find ETERNAL FIRE (*everlasting fire, eternal damnation*).

Here are the four times *eternal fire* (or *everlasting fire*) is used by the translators in the 1611 King James Version. Here is also where we uncover a mistranslation and misrepresentation of the original scriptures:

Wherefore if thy hand or thy foot offend thee, cut them off, and cast them from thee: it is better for thee to enter into life halt or maimed, rather than having two hands or two feet to be cast into EVERLASTING FIRE.
Matthew 18:8 - KJV

Then shall he say also unto them on the left hand, Depart from me, ye cursed, into EVERLASTING FIRE, prepared for the devil and his angels: For I was an hungred, and ye gave me no meat: I was thirsty, and ye gave me no drink: I was a stranger, and ye took me not in: naked, and ye clothed me not: sick, and in prison, and ye visited me not. Then shall they also answer him, saying, Lord, when saw we thee an hungred, or athirst, or a stranger, or naked, or sick, or in prison, and did not minister unto thee? Then shall he answer them, saying, Verily I say unto you, Inasmuch as ye did it not to one of the least of these, ye did it not to me. And these shall go away into EVERLASTING PUNISHMENT: but the righteous into life eternal.
Matthew 25:41-46 - KJV

Verily I say unto you, All sins shall be forgiven unto the sons of men, and blasphemies wherewith soever they shall blaspheme: But he that shall blaspheme against the Holy Ghost hath never forgiveness, but is in danger of ETERNAL DAMNATION.
Mark 3:28-29 - KJV

Even as Sodom and Gomorrha, and the cities about them in like manner, giving themselves over to fornication, and going after strange flesh, are set forth for an example, suffering the vengeance of ETERNAL FIRE.
Jude 1:7 - KJV

When the King James Bible uses the word *eternal* or *everlasting* it is actually the Greek word *aeon* from which we get the word *eon* which is translated *age*. In each of the four instances where the translators use the word *eternal* or *everlasting* it is literally in the Greek *age-abiding* or *age-during* (or age-enduring) judgment, purging or correction. Notice in these four passages taken from Young's Literal Translation that *eternal* or *everlasting fire* is seen more accurately as an *age-during* correction or purging:

*And if thy hand or thy foot doth cause thee to stumble, cut them off and cast from thee; it is good for thee to enter into the life lame or maimed, rather than having two hands or two feet, to be cast to the fire the **AGE-DURING**.*
Matthew 18:8 – Young's Literal Translation

*Then shall he say also to those on the left hand, Go ye from me, the cursed, to the fire, the **AGE-DURING**, that hath been prepared for the Devil and his messengers; for I did hunger, and ye gave me not to eat; I did thirst, and ye gave me not to drink;*

a stranger I was, and ye did not receive me; naked, and ye put not around me; infirm, and in prison, and ye did not look after me. Then shall they answer, they also, saying, Lord, when did we see thee hungering, or thirsting, or a stranger, or naked, or infirm, or in prison, and we did not minister to thee? Then shall he answer them, saying, Verily I say to you, Inasmuch as ye did [it] not to one of these, the least, ye did [it] not to me. And these shall go away to punishment **AGE-DURING**, *but the righteous to* life **AGE-DURING**.
Matthew 25:41-46 – Young's Literal Translation

Verily I say to you, that all the sins shall be forgiven to the sons of men, and evil speakings with which they might speak evil, but whoever may speak evil in regard to the Holy Spirit hath not forgiveness -- to the age, but is in danger of **AGE-DURING** judgment
Mark 3:28-29 – Young's Literal Translation

As Sodom and Gomorrah, and the cities around them, in like manner to these, having given themselves to whoredom, and gone after other flesh, have been set before -- an example, of fire **AGE-DURING**, *justice suffering.*
Jude 1:7 – Young's Literal Translation

In scripture, an *age* can be as brief as 3 days or even as long as a *generation*! However, *age* is never to be translated, or better mistranslated, as *eternal!*

Whatever our definition of hell (whether a literal place / a metaphor / a state of consciousness / now... or in the after life) let us be agreed that the nature of God is redemptive! We must be mindful that God will not *leave our soul in sheol (hell) Psalm 16:10.*

Now John answered and said, "Master, we saw someone casting out demons in Your name, and we forbade him because he does not follow with us."
But Jesus said to him, "Do not forbid him, for he who is not against us is on our side."
Now it came to pass, when the time had come for Him to be received up, that He steadfastly set His face to go to Jerusalem, and sent messengers before His face. And as they went, they entered a village of the SAMARITANS, to prepare for Him. But they did not receive Him, because His face was set for the journey to Jerusalem. And when His disciples James and John saw this, they said, "Lord, do You want us to command FIRE to come down from heaven and consume them, just as Elijah did?"
But He turned and rebuked them, and said, "You do not know what manner of spirit you are of. For the Son of Man did not come to destroy men's lives but to save them."
And they went to another village.
Luke 9:49-56 - NKJV

The fire of God is not designed to destroy men's lives…but to save them!

AFTER THE FIRE

We find a very interesting thought from David regarding the idea of an eternal fire or an eternal sentence to hell.

Where can I go from Your Spirit?
Or where can I flee from Your presence?
If I ascend into heaven, You are there;
If I make my bed in hell, behold, You are there.
Psalm 139:7-8 NKJV

Whether David is speaking of being in a literal or figurative hell we do not know. However, we can accurately gather that he was not there eternally. We also see that God did not send David to hell, but that David made (or chose) his own bed in hell. Finally, we find (similar to the story of the 3 Hebrew children in the fiery furnace) the reassurance that the presence of God was there in this hell with David.

In the last two chapters of the *book of Revelation* we stumble upon a very puzzling scenario concerning the *lake of fire* and those who are cast there. The same group that is cast into the *lake of fire* in chapter 21 is somehow strangely sitting outside of the gates of heaven in chapter 22.

But the cowardly, unbelieving, abominable, murderers, sexually
immoral, sorcerers, idolaters, and all liars shall have their part in
the lake which burns with fire and brimstone,
which is the second death.
Revelation 21:8 - NKJV

Blessed are those who wash their robes. They will be permitted to enter through the gates of the city and eat the fruit from the tree of life. Outside the city are the dogs—the sorcerers, the sexually immoral, the murderers, the idol worshipers, and all who love to live a lie.
Revelation 22:14-15 New Living

Again be mindful of the Greek translations regarding fire and brimstone (*Fire* – in the Greek is PUR – which is the root word for purify, purification, purge, purging, purgative, even Purgatory! *Brimstone* – in the Greek THEION from the root word *theos* which is translated divine, divinity, God-head, and Godlike!) The New Living Translation gives us more insight by letting us know that *brimstone* is actually the ancient word for *sulfur*, an active ingredient in most modern day medicines. Again, if we combine the words *fire and brimstone* we can accurately say the *PURGING OF GOD* is the process of purging that uncovers humanity's Godlikeness! Perhaps we can also now see that we are being medicated or treated in the *lake of sulfur* - not tortured.

The sexually immoral, murdering, lying group of people that were cast into the lake of fire is now out of the lake of fire and outside of the gates of the city. And what are they doing? They are waiting for the Spirit and the Bride to tell them to *COME IN!*

And the Spirit and the bride say, "Come!" And let him who hears say, "Come!" And let him who thirsts come. Whoever desires, let him take the water of life freely.
Revelation 22:17 - NKJV

I have always heard this passage preached in the dispensational context of the church inviting Jesus to return back to the earth. Notice that the earth is not the context here, but the city of heaven is what is being described. We understand this more accurately when we realize that those who are being invited to *Come* are thirsty and want to drink of the water of life. Jesus is not thirsty. Jesus does not need to drink of the water of life. Jesus is the Living Water of life.

So, who are the Spirit and the Bride talking to? They are talking to those who are outside the gates of the city; those who have been purged and purified in the lake of fire and are now thirsting for the water of life!

The Holy Bible of Inclusion

Part V ~ SEXUAL ORIENTATION

-INTRODUCTION-
✱

-CHALLENGES AND CHARGES-
✱

-BECOMING an INFORMED INCLUSIVE COMMUNITY-
(Revelation of the EUNUCH)
✱

-SLOPPY GRACE?-
✱

-THE SIN OF SODOM AND GOMORRAH-
✱

-LEVITICAL RELEVANCE-
✱

-THE BIBLE AS A WEAPON-
✱

-ROMANS 1-
✱

-I CORINTHIANS 6-
✱

-THE MINORITY OF TRUTH AND KINGIAN THEOLOGY-
✱

INTRODUCTION

Allow me to say at the outset of this teaching that the subject of homosexuality as it relates to the church is perhaps one of the most divisive and complicated issues to ever hit the church (and for that matter also civil rights and society in general). Whatever your personal opinion on this subject may be, all I ask of you while reading, is for you to try to avoid polarizing extremes of any sort. To be plain, God doesn't hate people...any people...gay or otherwise. God IS LOVE. On the other hand, the entire world is not gay and every professing heterosexual person is not secretly gay or somehow preoccupied with "homo-erotic" images and fantasies. Moderation and objectivity are required to maintain a healthy balance and a clear perspective. One thing is for sure, homosexuality is not a new issue, but an ancient one, and it isn't going anywhere. So, we must reason together sensibly and openly both to find the mind of God and to promote a tolerant, peaceful humanity.

Even at the end of biblical study and scientific research, there will still be some unsolved mysteries and unanswered questions surrounding this subject. In the final analysis **there may be some residing gray areas that can neither be ignored nor concluded upon, but should be viewed as a test of love and tolerance more than a contest of knowledge or scholarship.** Also, let us try to remember that sexuality is at best a temporary expression and not one worthy of carrying eternal weight or value. We are all eternal spirits having a temporary human experience.

Finally, I must admit that even though I am both student and teacher of the Bible I am not, and do not profess to be, a psychologist, geneticist, scientist or even a "sexpert." In short, sexuality is a very complex subject that cannot be understood through stereotype or any one set of eyes or opinions. Much that I will share on this subject will have scriptural foundation, historical biblical connection and implications. Yet, my own personal experience will shine through as well. With that said, *Come, let us REASON together!*

CHALLENGES AND CHARGES

Suicide, drug abuse, promiscuity and sexually transmitted diseases are some of the serious problems that plague both the heterosexual and homosexual communities. Are there gay men who are sexually promiscuous? Absolutely. Are there straight men who are sexually promiscuous? Absolutely. So, let us be cautious not to assign a stereotype of promiscuity to a specific group that may equally exist outside of that specific group. In my own opinion, the greater problems facing the gay community are more fundamental and not merely symptomatic. *Proverbs 29:15* - tells us that a *child left to himself brings his mother to shame.* For the most part, the church in general has left the gay community to itself, both consciously and unconsciously, by way of calculated rejection, neglectful abandonment and outright prejudice and hatred. If there is any behavior that seems to be "shameful," the mother (the church) must at very least bear her share of responsibility and shame.

Charges against Homosexuals:

1) They are *sick* and need to be healed or *delivered.*

Despite the perhaps well-intentioned efforts of the church to *deliver* people from being gay, most never lose their attraction for the same sex. Even if they FORCE THEMSELVES and their bodies to physically live as a heterosexual, the mind remains homosexual. It is noteworthy that many gay people love God so deeply and sincerely that they are willing to go through numerous humiliating public attempts to be *changed* in an effort to retain their accepted status in their church family; to remain a part of their biological family and to be obedient to what they perceive is God's command. I am not personally convinced that it would be possible for a *sick*, mentally deranged or demon possessed person (in the past and presently religious groups have labeled gay people as such) to exhibit this degree of love for God and care for family.

Put simply, a left-handed person cannot be *delivered* from being left-handed anymore than a red-headed person can be *healed* of being red-headed. However, a left-handed person can force himself to write with his right hand and a red-headed person can dye her hair another color. But, the left-handed person will always be left-handed and the red-headed person will always be red-headed. Forcing people (gay or otherwise) to live against their nature eventually and inevitably creates an environment replete with falsehoods and perversions (which we see rampant in the modern Christian church).

Interestingly enough, about ten percent of the world's population is either left handed or red-headed. And yes, about ten percent of the world is gay. It is not unnatural to be left-handed or red-headed, even though it may be abnormal or other than the norm. Abnormal and unnatural are not synonymous. In the animal kingdom, specifically among the higher mammals, same gender sexual attraction and even devotion has been studied for years and is neither uncommon nor rare. Perhaps this 10% is a tithe – a holy mystery belonging wholly to God alone?

Furthermore, no human male is completely void of estrogen (female hormone). No human female is completely void of testosterone (male hormone). However, over time all males produce less testosterone and all females produce less estrogen (thus we become less different and more alike as we age. Similar to the natural aging process, as we mature spiritually we become less divided and connect more closely to Spirit).

Notice in this next passage that Paul explains beautifully the process of human devolution and spiritual evolution. As the temporary fades away, the eternal is revealed. As the natural body diminishes, the spiritual body is magnified.

If there is a natural body, there is also a spiritual body. So it is written: "The first man Adam became a living being"; the last Adam, a life-giving spirit. The spiritual did not come first, but the natural, and after that the spiritual. The first man was of the dust of the earth, the second man from heaven. As was the earthly man, so are those who are of the earth; and as is the man from heaven, so also are those who are of heaven. And just as we have borne the likeness of the earthly man, so shall we bear the likeness of the man from heaven.
I Corinthians 15:44-49 - NIV

In other words, as we grow older we are less of a sexual being and we begin to become more of a "life-giving spirit."

To avoid a state of polarization among groups with differing opinions, at least in this limited physical realm of consciousness and expression, let us consider the idea that if someone is "born" heterosexual (if we can completely and accurately know this as a fact) and has by whatever path arrived in a homosexual lifestyle, they can and should be allowed to reconnect with their true self, natural orientation and original sexual expression. However, if someone is "born" homosexual (if we can completely and accurately know this as a fact) and has by whatever means arrived in a false, disingenuous and unnatural heterosexual lifestyle, they can and should be allowed to be their true authentic self – and not be forced to be an imposter for the sake of social status or religious respectability.

2) They are *sinful* and need to be forgiven.

Please allow me to be clear here, I offer the following scenario only in an attempt to speak to every angle of this issue. Personally, I do not subscribe to the idea that homosexuality is a sin, and I will give a plethora of scripture (and personal experience) later in this section to support this most controversial opinion.

Jesus replied, "Moses permitted you to divorce your wives because your hearts were hard. But it was not this way from the beginning. I tell you that anyone who divorces his wife, except for marital unfaithfulness, and marries another woman commits adultery."
Matthew 19:8-9 NIV

Anyone who divorces his wife and marries another woman commits adultery, and the man who marries a divorced woman commits adultery.
Luke 16:18 – NIV (also refer to Mark 10; Matthew 5)

IF homosexuality is a sin, Jesus never speaks of it as such, yet he does speak harshly against divorce and remarriage. Today, well over fifty percent of Christians, or followers of Christ, are divorced and many are remarried. Ironically, many of the pastors who speak against they gay community while citing scripture as their justification are divorced and remarried themselves. In essence, we have rejected what Jesus never discussed, and accepted what Jesus spoke against.

However, in an effort to be thorough and to avoid estranging people who will surely cite the following scriptures, yes the book of Leviticus does say for a man to lie with a man as with a woman is an *abomination* and the first chapter of Romans does refer to homosexuality as a result of being *unthankful, disobedient to parents, hating God* and other causes. I Timothy and I Corinthians make mention in a similar manner. Later in this section we will discuss at length and in context the references to homosexuality in each of these books. For the sake of argument, let us hypothetically consider the notion for a moment that being gay is a sin.

IF being gay is a sin, is it any different or "worse" than any other sin?

If you really keep the royal law found in Scripture, "Love your neighbor as yourself," you are doing right. BUT IF YOU SHOW FAVORITISM, YOU SIN AND ARE CONVICTED BY THE LAW AS LAWBREAKERS. FOR WHOEVER KEEPS THE WHOLE LAW AND YET STUMBLES AT JUST ONE POINT IS GUILTY OF BREAKING ALL OF IT. For he who said, "Do not commit adultery," also said, "Do not murder." If you do not commit adultery but do commit murder, you have become a lawbreaker. Speak and act as those who are going to be judged by the law that gives freedom, because judgment without mercy will be shown to anyone who has not been merciful. Mercy triumphs over judgment!
James 2:8-13 NIV

The writer James makes it clear to us that the very act of esteeming one sin over another or showing *favoritism* toward one person causes us to become *lawbreakers*. Furthermore, if we break just one law we are guilty of breaking all of them! So we must be careful and conscious of how we compare one sin over and against another sin. For instance, many anointed gospel preachers and singers are not merely overweight, but obese and even gluttoness (gluttony is listed as one of the *seven deadly sins* that God hates). Yet, we celebrate this condition as a part of the accepted church culture. How is one sin celebrated, or at very least tolerated, while another is seen as abominable?

If we claim to be without sin, we deceive ourselves and the truth is not in us. If we confess our sins, he is faithful and just and will forgive us our sins and purify us from all unrighteousness. IF WE CLAIM WE HAVE NOT SINNED, we make him out to be a liar and his word has no place in our lives.
I John 1:8-10 NIV

IF being gay is a sin, it must not be viewed scripturally as being better or worse than any other sin. Further, we have *ALL sinned (in the past) and FALL short (in the present and future) of God's glory (Romans 3:23)*. Therefore, we must ALL be mindful and willing to accurately apply an even amount of value to every sin, both to our own and to the sin of others. We ALL have sinned in the past and will ALL sin in the future. Sin is sin. It ALL weighs the same. And Jesus carried ALL of it to the cross.

> *Behold the Lamb of God that takes away the SIN (hamartia) of the world.*
> ### *John 1:29 - NKJV*

> *My dear children, I write this to you so that you will not SIN (hamartano). But if anybody does sin, we have one who speaks to the Father in our defense—Jesus Christ, the Righteous One. He is the atoning sacrifice for our sins, and not only for ours but also for the sins of the WHOLE WORLD.*
> ### *I John 2:1-2 - NIV*

The word SIN used here in the Greek is *hamartia*, which simply means *OFFENSE*. Because of Christ and the finished work of Calvary, we can no longer OFFEND God. However, after Christ, we do still sin. Don't we? Yes. Even though our *hamartia*, or our offense has been washed away, our *hamartano*, which in the Greek means *MISSING THE MARK*, still remains a potential possibility and perhaps an inevitability. If we miss the mark, Jesus speaks in our defense as the atoning sacrifice for all sin, and not only for us, but also for the *WHOLE WORLD!* In the end, if anyone is absolutely and unalterably convinced that homosexuality is a sin, then there is Good News; because of Jesus, it does not and cannot offend God (even if it is a missing of the mark). The Good News is that Jesus paid it all.

But where sin increased, grace increased all the more.
Romans 5:20 - NIV

3) They are a threat to society (marriage, family, church, community).

To speak rationally (whether you believe homosexuality is a sin or not) I am not sure the gay community is to be blamed for the deterioration of heterosexual marriages. My ability, tendency and inclination to be a heterosexual man, husband and father is not tampered with in any way by the gay community. Further, if gay people are a threat to the church we must ask ourselves the question, "What would our worship experience be without the contribution from the gay community? Musically? Artistically? Aesthetically?" The gay community's ability to renovate dilapidated buildings and to revive crime-ridden neighborhoods is above question or criticism. Beauty does not spring forth from the well of ugly!

4) They demand special rights.

I have never heard of any religious, political or social activist gay organization demanding special rights. We must make a distinction here between equal rights and special rights. To voice the desire to be treated as a human, equal to other humans, or even as an American taxpaying citizen, does not necessarily mean a group is demanding special rights.

We hold these truths to be self-evident, that all men are created equal, that they are endowed by their Creator with certain unalienable Rights, that among these are Life, Liberty and the pursuit of Happiness.
Thomas Jefferson – Declaration of Independence

5) They are ungodly.

The word ungodly simply means *irreligious*. I am not in the least convinced that gay people are irreligious. On the contrary, I have found that churches everywhere (both gay friendly and not) are full of gay people desirous to offer unto God their worship, gifts, talents, time and money! If there are differing opinions of God's plan for pro-creation, then let us reserve that argument or line of thinking to a specific conversation and subject. But, to assert that the entire gay community is ungodly, irreligious, without thought or worship or love for God is a dangerous, destructive and divisive generalization.

Gay worshipers who attend non-inclusive churches may prove this point the greatest. How? They sit week after week, and at times endure prejudice and belittlement, all in an effort to be a part of the Body of Christ and to be in the presence of God. A thirst for God that is willing to endure this type of treatment cannot be categorized as being ungodly or as irreligious.

6) Homosexuality is a result of molestation, a passive father or a domineering mother.

Is being gay more about *nature* or *nurture*? Is a person born gay? Or does a specific environment tend to make a heterosexual person gay? This question may be better dealt with later when we look at Jesus' teaching in Matthew 19. Here Jesus says of the *eunuchs,* or asexual males, that there are some who were *made* eunuchs by men. To be thorough, many people living a gay lifestyle were sexually molested in some way as a child. Yet, there are just as many or more who were never molested; who did not have a weak father and an overbearing mother; they are just gay. Again, sexuality is a very complicated subject. On a scale from 1 to 10 (1 being the *most* gay and 10 being the *most* straight) there are very few people who could be categorized as a 1 or a 10. As I noted earlier, every male has some presence of the female hormone estrogen, and every female has some presence of the male hormone testosterone. Many people have a strong sexual preference for the opposite sex while maintaining a healthy appreciation for the same sex.

Let me reiterate, if someone is heterosexual by orientation (nature) but for any number of reasons (nurture) has been living a gay lifestyle, we should provide a safe and loving environment to allow them to recapture their authentic true self once again. However, if there are homosexuals by orientation (nature) that are living any lifestyle that is not in keeping with their true authentic self (nurture), we must provide a safe and loving environment to allow them to recapture their true authentic gay self once again.

7) Homosexuality is contagious.

Not contagious. If it is, I would surely have "caught gay" by now (considering how many gay friends and family members I have). The truth is that being around gay people cannot make a heterosexual become gay (but perhaps a bit more fashion conscious).

Personally, I have found in many cases that the more homophobic a person is, the more unsure that person may be of his or her own sexuality. As Shakespeare once wrote: *Me thinks thou dost protest too much!*

BECOMING AN INFORMED INCLUSIVE COMMUNITY (REVELATION OF THE EUNUCH)

If we are to use the Bible as a foundation for God's love and inclusion of all people, how do we deal with the six or seven scriptures that seem to condemn or speak against homosexuality?

Allow me to present three key scriptures as we embark on a scriptural study of this subject (Matthew 19, Isaiah 56 and Acts 8):

Jesus replied, "Not everyone can accept this word, but only those to whom it has been given. For some are eunuchs because they were BORN THAT WAY; others were made that way by men; and others have renounced marriage because of the kingdom of heaven. The one who can accept this should accept it."
Matthew 19:11-12 NIV

First of all, let us establish what Jesus meant by *eunuch*. A eunuch was a male who had been castrated for several purposes (eunuchs were created by men for the purpose of protecting the king's harem of women without being a threat sexually). Eunuchs also served many different roles in the religious temples. A eunuch was not necessarily a gay man. Yet, a eunuch also was no longer a heterosexual male, but asexual or without sexual expression. Apparently, in Jesus' day there arose a question concerning eunuchs. The response of Jesus reveals the complexity of sexuality. Jesus says that there are actually three different types of eunuchs:

1-Eunuchs who are BORN THAT WAY
2-Eunuchs who are MADE that way by men
3-And Eunuchs who have RENOUNCED marriage for the kingdom

Categories two and three are neither surprising nor unexpected - *made* that way by men and *chose* to be that way for the Kingdom (nurture). Yet, the first category requires quite a bit of thought – *BORN THAT WAY* (nature). Now, to be accurate, Jesus did not say that these eunuchs were *born* gay. However, He did say that they were born as other than heterosexual or born as asexual or castrated males. This is both significant and mysterious. Why? Because it speaks specifically to the age-old debate of "Nature versus Nurture." *BORN THAT WAY* sheds a different light on the idea that every gay person either *chooses* to be gay or is *conditioned* to be gay by their environment or by the nurturing they received.

According to Jesus, if some eunuchs are *BORN* asexual then it is highly likely that there is gray area in regards to sexual orientation and expression. If a person is *BORN* as other than heterosexual, do we continue the attempts to change or *deliver* them from what is their authentic nature? If some people are *BORN* as *other* than heterosexual, should they live less than an abundant life? Or do they not have a valid right to the promises of God?

Let no foreigner who has bound himself to the LORD say, "The LORD will surely exclude me from his people." And let not any EUNUCH complain, "I am only a dry tree." For this is what the LORD says: "To the eunuchs who keep my Sabbaths, who choose what pleases me and hold fast to my covenant - to them I will give WITHIN MY TEMPLE AND ITS WALLS a memorial and a name better than sons and daughters; I will give them an everlasting name that will not be cut off.
Isaiah 56:3-5 NIV

In the 8th Chapter of Acts Philip encounters a eunuch who was treasurer for the Ethiopian Queen Candace. Notice the details around this exchange: the eunuch has gone to Jerusalem to worship; was reading the book of Isaiah (specifically about the coming of

Jesus); invites Philip to explain the scriptures in Isaiah referring to Jesus; hears the Good News and desires to be baptized; God seals this encounter with the miraculous.

Now an angel of the Lord said to Philip, "Go south to the road— the desert road—that goes down from Jerusalem to Gaza." So he started out, and on his way he met an Ethiopian EUNUCH, an important official in charge of all the treasury of Candace, queen of the Ethiopians. This man had gone to Jerusalem to worship, and on his way home was sitting in his chariot reading the book of Isaiah the prophet. The Spirit told Philip, "Go to that chariot and stay near it." Then Philip ran up to the chariot and heard the man reading Isaiah the prophet. "Do you understand what you are reading?" Philip asked.
"How can I," he said, "unless someone explains it to me?" So he invited Philip to come up and sit with him. The eunuch was reading this passage of Scripture: "He was led like a sheep to the slaughter, and as a lamb before the shearer is silent, so he did not open his mouth. In his humiliation he was deprived of justice. Who can speak of his descendants For his life was taken from the earth."
The eunuch asked Philip, "Tell me, please, who is the prophet talking about, himself or someone else?" Then Philip began with that very passage of Scripture and told him the good news about Jesus.
As they traveled along the road, they came to some water and the eunuch said, "Look, here is water. Why shouldn't I be baptized?" And he gave orders to stop the chariot. THEN BOTH PHILIP AND THE EUNUCH WENT DOWN INTO THE WATER AND PHILIP BAPTIZED HIM. When they came up out of the water, the Spirit of the Lord suddenly took Philip away, and the eunuch did not see him again, but went on his way rejoicing. Philip, however, appeared at Azotus and traveled about, preaching the gospel in all the towns until he reached Caesarea.
Acts 8:26-40 - NIV

SLOPPY GRACE?

As we continue our discussion of sexual orientation let us not be naïve to the charges against an inclusive biblical perspective and expression. Many who do not share this perspective make the accusation that Inclusive Theology is based upon a *permissive* or *sloppy* grace that merely winks at issues like promiscuity and infidelity. Another charge is that this brand of inclusivity is embraced only by churches that have morally corrupt leadership; and who are merely attempting to justify their own misguided conduct and irresponsible behavior by preaching a loose theology.

Let us be clear, sloppy grace has no place in Inclusion. If people make poor choices there will be consequences for those choices. Sowing and reaping, seedtime and harvest, action and reaction, karma, thermodynamics – these are universal laws that must be understood and respected. If we choose to use an Inclusive Gospel as a means for justifying a careless life, we do so at our own peril. *God is Love.* God's *Mercy endures forever.* Yet, we can either realize peace or chaos in this lifetime. Remember, eternal life is given to all. However, abundant life is the result of Kingdom living.

For example, although polygamy is biblically debatable and can be clearly seen throughout the Old Testament even in the lives of leaders whom God anoints, at present monogamy seems to be the safest choice sexually and emotionally in this physical dimension of reality. We must be cautious, or better, conscious to not allow our *good to be evil spoken of.* In short, whatever our life experience may be, we must be mature enough to preach and declare the finished work of a victorious Christ while simultaneously embracing the standards, and attempting to live by the example, that Christ set for us. Gay Christians, and Straight Christians alike, should strive to live a life of moral responsibility, biblical holiness and complete submission to God.

THE SIN OF SODOM AND GOMORRAH

To be objective and unbiased, no matter how we spin it or explain it, the Bible does seem (at least on the surface) to speak harshly against homosexuality. However, we must be able to understand the culture and context that these verses were written in and ask ourselves how they apply to the entire Bible, and how they apply to us today. When we *rightly divide* the events and lessons from the Genesis account of Sodom and Gomorrah we are left to ponder several questions:

➢ What was the SIN of Sodom and Gomorrah?

➢ Was it specifically homosexuality? Or was it an uncontrolled lust for all things pleasurable?

From the biblical account in Genesis, we can safely derive that the standards to which Sodom and Gomorrah held, both sexually and socially, were displeasing to God and inhospitable toward men; specifically foreigners.

Let us recount the details that led to the destruction of Sodom and Gomorrah from the 19th chapter of Genesis:

➢ Two angels, disguised as foreign human men, enter the city of Sodom and at Lot's request decide to stay the night with Lot and his family.

➢ Not long after these angels enter Lot's house the men of Sodom come to the house *demanding* Lot to release them so that they might have sex with them.

> Lot attempts to detour the men with other sexual offers (his virgin daughters) but the men *insist* on having sex with Lot's guests.

> The men of Sodom become so persistent that the disguised angels in Lot's house strike the men of Sodom with blindness.

> There is no record of the men of Sodom continuing to pursue after becoming blind. However, there is still a sense in the story of Lot's family and guests being in danger for the remainder of the night.

Whatever your opinion of homosexuality or of this story, what we can clearly see here is men who are completely out of control sexually; men who take no consideration of how their actions might affect or impose upon others. The pressuring, insistence and demanding that is seen in these men of Sodom shows both a lack of control and a lack of concern for anything other than their own desires. Ezekiel gives us a glimpse of how this *Sodom* mindset of uncontrolled lusts and desires leads to a life replete with selfishness, greed and social (or even sexual) irresponsibility.

Now this was the sin of your sister Sodom: She and her daughters
were arrogant, overfed and unconcerned;
they did not help the poor and needy.
Ezekiel 16:49 – NIV

Notice, Ezekiel does not focus on any specific type of sexual act, but rather directs our attention to the harsh result of a life full of seeking only pleasure and selfish desire without concern for others; specifically the poor and needy. If arrogance, overindulgence and lack of concern for the needy were the sins of Sodom, are there expressions of this type of sin today in the churches that preach against the gay community? The sin of Sodom and Gomorrah cannot be limited to a sexual expression, but must, at the very least, be broadened to include being arrogant, overeating and having a lack of social consciousness.

Jesus actually speaks of a level of *tolerance* being shown for Sodom and Gomorrah on the *day of judgment* because they were not exposed to the miraculous power of God as were the people of His day (Matthew 10 and 11; Luke 10 and 17). Perhaps this tolerance Jesus speaks of is the *lake of fire, fire and brimstone* (fire from the Greek "pur" - to purge or purify; brimstone from the Greek "theon" - meaning God) or the *fire of God*. In other words, because God is purgative, not punitive, there may be a season where God mercifully purges the flesh of man to reveal the spirit of man.

> *As Sodom and Gomorrah, and the cities around them, in like manner to these, having given themselves to whoredom, and gone after other flesh, have been set before - an example, of fire AGE-DURING, justice suffering.*
> **Jude 1:7 – Young's Literal Translation**

Here in the book of Jude we see that there will be an *AGE-DURING* or *temporary purging* by God to purify people who are controlled by their flesh or who have given themselves over to unrestraint. The prophet Amos confirms this by showing that God's desire is not to destroy with fire, but to purge people for a season to be restored. Yet, some seem to have a need to be in this purging for a longer period of time than others. Thus, we must embrace in our lives the lessons that the fire of God comes to teach us, and embrace them quickly.

190

I overthrew some of you as I overthrew Sodom and Gomorrah. You were like a burning stick SNATCHED FROM THE FIRE...
Amos 4:11 - NIV

Notice that Amos makes it clear that we are not in the fire eternally. But rather, we are *SNATCHED FROM THE FIRE.*

Presently, society (and segments of the Christian church alike) is guilty of the sin of Sodom and Gomorrah (arrogance, overeating, overindulgence, inhospitality to strangers, uncontrolled sexual desire and a lack of care for the needy) and is in need of righteous men and women to be as salt and light influencing the hearts and minds of those who have lost touch with their Spirit. Sodom and Gomorrah need us! Remember, the day Lot left Sodom, and Abraham ceased to intercede for Sodom, the cities of Sodom and Gomorrah were destroyed (Luke 17:29).

LEVITICAL RELEVANCE

If a man lies with a man as one lies with a woman, both of them have done what is detestable. They must be put to death.
Leviticus 20:13 - NIV

On the surface this seems pretty cut and dry – two men being together sexually is unacceptable to God. However, we must dig deeper in order to rightly divide the Word of Truth and to find the whole counsel of God. First, we must establish that Leviticus is full of hundreds of holiness codes that we ignore daily in modern times and further that are no longer relevant today or applicable for New Covenant adherers (i.e. Peter's vision of the unclean animals). Also, according to Jesus, if we are to be justified by the law we must keep all of the law. Jesus was very clear on this point, if we break one commandment it's as if we have broken them all! So, with respect to biblical accuracy and application, we cannot single out one Levitical law while ignoring the others (refer to *I Don't Know... the Way of Knowing* pgs. 224-225).

For instance, these are just a few of the laws in Leviticus and Exodus, that if broken, the punishment is execution either by burning or stoning:

➤ Having sex with wife during monthly period of menstruation – Leviticus 15:19-24

➤ Approaching the altar with any sight defect – Leviticus 21:20

➤ Men cutting the hair around their temples – Leviticus 19:27

➤ Touching the skin of a dead pig – Leviticus 11:6-8

➢ Working on the Sabbath - Exodus 35:2

➢ Eating scavengers (shrimp, crab, lobster, oyster, scallop, clam, muscle, conch) -Leviticus 11:10

Leviticus also says we are to stone a son who is not working and prohibits tattoos, planting more than one crop in a field, wearing garments of more than one fabric and having sex with or marrying an in-law. Speaking of marrying an in-law, Judah, the son of Jacob, married and had children with Tamar, the widow of his deceased son – further, all of this is mentioned in the lineage of Jesus (*Judah the father of Perez and Zerah, whose mother was Tamar...Matthew 1:3 – NIV*).

Genesis even speaks of God slaying a man named Onan because he *spilled his seed (semen) on the ground* – Genesis 38:9-10. From this one scripture many absolutists have taught that masturbation is a sin. But when we continue to research the *culture and context* behind this line of thinking we find that in Onan's day it was commonly held that a man's semen contained the *whole of life* and needed no female egg or ovulation. Therefore, masturbation was considered to be murder and punishable by execution. Today, science has revealed to us more knowledge - and with this knowledge we must accurately apply appropriate modifications to the scripture and to its application. Similarly, a recent study from Canada in 2007, revealed that Lesbian women respond very much like heterosexual men when psychologically examined. This is why every scripture must be read with consideration to the context and culture of the time in which it was written.

These examples are not aimed at justifying homosexuality – but rather designed to shine a light on the hypocrisy of seeing the world, and attempting to interpret the Bible, in black and white or in absolute, literal, concrete terms.

I am not aware of any Christian person or religious figure who literally follows every one of the 600-plus Levitical laws and holiness codes, but many use a few verses found in Leviticus as a weapon against the gay community.

THE BIBLE AS A WEAPON

We must use caution when attempting to use the Bible as a weapon against any group. If we insist on using the Bible as a weapon we must be prepared if and when the weapon we use to inflict hurt is turned toward and used against us (*as the Word of God is a TWO-EDGED sword*). Jesus told Peter not to live by the sword for danger of dying by the sword (John 18).

Let's look at how the Bible has been used throughout history by vicious and hateful people as a weapon to promote bigotry and to further marginalize minorities and oppress the disenfranchised:

The Bible has been used to justify possessing, purchasing and punishing Slaves:

And you may take them as an inheritance for your children after you, to inherit them AS A POSSESSION; they shall be your permanent slaves. But regarding your brethren, the children of Israel, you shall not rule over one another with rigor.
Leviticus 25:46 – NIV

And if one of your brethren who dwells by you becomes poor, and sells himself to you, you shall not compel him to serve as a slave.
Leviticus 25:39 - NIV

It is interesting that this same chapter in Leviticus both promotes and discourages slavery.

The PROMOTION – to make slaves of those who are not your Hebrew brethren.

The DISCOURAGEMENT – to treat a Hebrew brother as a slave.

This line of thinking also uncovers to us a very racist strain in the book of Leviticus. In other words (according to Leviticus), slavery is okay as long as you don't make a Hebrew a slave.

These next 5 passages are not meant to cause hurt – but simply to remind us that the Bible can be used (and used accurately) for very hurtful purposes.

SLAVES, OBEY YOUR EARTHLY MASTERS with respect and fear, and with sincerity of heart, JUST AS YOU WOULD OBEY CHRIST.
Ephesians 6:5 - NIV

Slaves, obey your earthly masters in everything; and do it, not only when their eye is on you and to win their favor, but with sincerity of heart and REVERENCE FOR THE LORD.
Colossians 3:22 - NIV

All who are under the yoke of slavery should CONSIDER THEIR MASTERS WORTHY OF FULL RESPECT, so that God's name and our teaching may not be slandered.
I Timothy 6:1 - NIV

Teach slaves to be subject to their masters in everything, to try to please them, not to talk back to them.
Titus 2:9 - NIV

*Slaves, submit yourselves to your masters with all respect, NOT
ONLY TO THOSE WHO ARE GOOD AND CONSIDERATE,
BUT ALSO TO THOSE WHO ARE HARSH.*
I Peter 2:18 – NIV

No one would agree that slavery is godly or justifiable in the modern
era (at least we all hope not). Yet, Paul and Peter specifically
encourage slaves to *obey* and serve their masters (even the *harsh*
ones) and to obey and serve them with *reverence* as if it were
an offering to God and as an act of preservation of *God's name!*
However, every day we refuse to act in accordance with these
scriptures because we know deep in our hearts (no matter what the
Bible may say on this issue) that no human being, regardless of race,
should ever be treated as anything less than a child of God.

Unfortunately, many who reject these scriptures regarding slavery
(on the grounds that they are both archaic and offensive) do not
use the same consciousness in regards to the scriptures that are
demeaning and offensive to homosexuals.

Abraham and Solomon both utilized slaves for their own benefit
and purposes also. Were Abraham, Solomon, Peter and Paul all
completely wrong about slavery and its oppressive foundations,
implications and applications – but somehow completely right about
oppressing homosexuals?

The Bible has been used for the Denigration of Women:

*As in ALL THE CONGREGATIONS of the saints, WOMEN
SHOULD REMAIN SILENT IN THE CHURCHES. THEY ARE
NOT ALLOWED TO SPEAK, but must be in submission, as the
Law says. If they want to inquire about something, they should ask*

their own husbands at home; FOR IT IS DISGRACEFUL FOR A
WOMAN TO SPEAK IN THE CHURCH.
I Corinthians 14:33-35 – NIV

Although this passage is very clear about the restrictions that are to be placed upon women in all congregations and in all church services (not only the churches and services in Rome) most Christian churches completely disregard this verse and openly allow women to speak, and even teach, preach and prophesy, during worship services. Why? Because none of us can deny when a person is truly gifted and anointed by God (male or female) and because we consider this an outdated mode of thinking. However, if a musician, songwriter or even preacher is honest about their same gender attraction and orientation, they are usually asked to step down from ministry and many times even encouraged to leave the church completely.

Adolf Hitler used the Bible as support for the Jewish Holocaust:

Pilate said to them, "What then shall I do with Jesus who is called
Christ?" They all said to him, "Let Him be crucified!" Then the
governor said, "Why, what evil has He done?"
But they cried out all the more, saying, "Let Him be crucified!"
When Pilate saw that he could not prevail at all, but rather that a
tumult was rising, he took water and washed his hands before the
multitude, saying, "I am innocent of the blood of this just Person.
You see to it."
And all the people answered and said, "HIS BLOOD BE ON US
AND ON OUR CHILDREN."
Matthew 27:22-25 - NKJV

When the Bible records that the Jewish Priests, Elders and people agreed to reap the consequence of crucifying Jesus *(His blood be on us and our children)* – Hitler chose to use this verse as a means for biblically justifying his attempt to exterminate the Jewish people altogether.

In retrospect, we look back at these moments in history and we are utterly ashamed of man's inhumanity to man. We build museums and exhibits that carefully document the awful details and personal stories associated with these atrocities. In these halls of shame we can usually find the words "Never Again!" We read quotes such as "If we do not know our history…we are doomed to repeat it!" Yet, even though we leave these places deeply moved, even tearful, do we ever ask the most pressing and appropriate question, "Is society, or the church, presently oppressing another group of humanity that will cause us to be ashamed in the future?" If we do not ask this question we are only doomed to repeat the shame associated historically with those who have used the BIBLE AS A WEAPON. Historically, and tragically, the Bible has been used in this manner by evil men and against innocent people.

Here are just a few examples of how the Bible has been misused to support man's inhumanity to man:

…to prove *The Divine Right of Kings* – (the Magna Carta won and the Bible lost).

…to prosecute *Copernicus, Galileo* – (Science won and the Bible lost).

…to condemn *The Divorced* – (Reason won and the Bible lost).

…to justify *Racial Discrimination and Segregation in America* – (Justice won and the Bible lost).

…to persecute *The Gay Community* – (Truth will win and the Bible will lose).

Any time the Bible is used as a weapon against an oppressed people it is being used inappropriately. Biblical literalists must remember that the *letter (or literal) kills, but the Spirit gives life.*

ROMANS 1

One of the arguments for the exclusion of gay people in the Christian church is that the Apostle Paul, in the New Testament, condemns this lifestyle. So, let us dig deeper into this passage to find the culture, context and hidden truths. First, the church in Rome was positioned culturally in an environment where sexual expression had become a part of their worship and the human body had become an object of worship and deified. Second, be aware that Paul was addressing a group of Christians that had been engulfed in and exposed to a culture that had built temples to Aphrodite and Diana, the fertility gods and goddesses of sexual passion. Sexual orgies and temple prostitutes were all part of the ceremonial worship of their deities. As we examine this passage, remember that Paul is already set on edge because of the excess of sexual promiscuity. Finally, try to process the thought that Paul is not addressing monogamous gay couples who love God and live a standard of commitment to a single partner. He is addressing a general group of people who had cast off any form of control or sexual responsibility.

Because of this, God gave them over to shameful lusts. Even their women exchanged natural relations for unnatural ones. In the same way the men also abandoned natural relations with women and were inflamed with lust for one another. Men committed indecent acts with other men, and received in themselves the due penalty for their perversion.
Romans 1:26-27 – NIV

Because of "THIS" what? We have to read in context the entire story to find out what "THIS" is.

For although they knew God, they neither glorified him as God nor gave thanks to him, but their thinking became futile and their foolish hearts were darkened.
Romans 1:21 - NIV

"THIS" represents people who would not glorify God nor give thanks to God. Consider a few questions here. Do the gay members of our churches refuse to glorify God? Do they refuse to thank God? Furthermore, referring back to v.26-27 have our gay members *exchanged* their passion for the opposite sex or were they *born* homosexual? Let's consider vs. 28-31…

Furthermore, since they did not think it worthwhile to retain the knowledge of God, he gave them over to a depraved mind, to do what ought not to be done. They have become filled with every kind of wickedness, evil, greed and depravity. They are full of envy, murder, strife, deceit and malice. They are gossips, slanderers, God-haters, insolent, arrogant and boastful; they invent ways of doing evil; they disobey their parents; they are senseless, faithless, heartless, ruthless.
Romans 1:28-31 - NIV

Do our gay members not think a knowledge of God is worth retaining? Then why do they come week after week to hear from God and to gain a greater knowledge of God? Are our gay members greedy? Murderous? God-haters? Disobedient to parents? Faithless and heartless?

I CORINTHIANS 6

Do you not know that the wicked will not inherit the kingdom of God? Do not be deceived: Neither the sexually immoral nor idolaters nor adulterers nor male prostitutes nor homosexual offenders nor thieves nor the greedy nor drunkards nor slanderers nor swindlers will inherit the kingdom of God. And that is what some of you were. But you were washed, you were sanctified, you were justified in the name of the Lord Jesus Christ and by the Spirit of our God.
I Corinthians 6:9-11 -NIV

The Greek word *maloakoi* used here for homosexual is "effeminate" or "male prostitutes." Although many gay men may exhibit some degree of feminine energy there are just as many gay men who are as masculine as any heterosexual man. And, it should go without saying, that we certainly should not confuse or group male prostitutes or "call boys" with committed monogamous gay men, gay people or gay couples.

Furthermore, because of the blood of Christ, even this group of male prostitutes has been *washed, and sanctified and justified!* Those who live as male prostitutes may make their *bed in hell* on this earth (or perhaps it was made in hell for them?), but they are every bit as reconciled to God as is the rest of the world.

THE MINORITY OF TRUTH AND KINGIAN THEOLOGY

"Even if you are A Minority of ONE – the Truth is still the Truth!"
Mahatma Gandhi

A minority of one with truth is much greater than a majority of many with untruth! Historically, the Majority has been wrong on many social and religious issues. Allow me give a few examples of those who had a Minority of Truth:

➢ **Jesus the Christ** – challenged the majority's view of God, race, religion, law and love.

➢ **Abraham Lincoln** – challenged the majority's view on slavery and equality.

➢ **Martin Luther King, Jr.** – challenged the majority's view on discrimination, segregation, Civil and Human Rights.

All of these men were killed for their truth, a minority of truth. Yet, we (the majority) now walk unencumbered on the trails that they gave their lives to blaze. The majority always enjoys the freedoms that a minority pays for. If you find comfort and safety in the majority – you may end up comfortably and safely on the wrong side of history! Living in the minority of truth may lessen the amount of friends that you have. However, the friends that you retain will be people of power, purpose and passion. You may be estranged, and even excommunicated, but you will be in good company.

"It's an evil day when good men keep silent."
Dr. Martin Luther King, Jr.

*"It's not the words of my enemies that I remember,
but the silence of my friends."*
Dr. Martin Luther King, Jr.

*"What affects one directly affects all indirectly... Injustice
anywhere is a threat to justice everywhere."*
Dr. Martin Luther King, Jr.

I am heterosexual. I am male. I am American. I am Caucasian. These are my earthly, given labels. These are the sexual, gender, cultural and racial orientations that I was born into. Why should I care for anyone who exists, or struggles, outside of my orientations? Because I am connected to all of mankind. And, if I were marginalized and disenfranchised by the simple incident of my birth, I would want someone in the majority to speak up and on my behalf!

Part VI - END TIMES
(from a Scriptural Perspective)

―◆―

-THE LIKE — AS PRINCIPLE-

✳

-THE DANGER IN LITERALISM (the Antichrist)-

✳

-SETTING DATES-

✳

-THE GOSPEL OF THE KINGDOM-

✳

-JESUS ALREADY RETURNED…AT PENTECOST-

✳

-SPECIALNESS-

✳

Again let me say to all making this journey that very few of us, if any, will see ideas of spirituality identically or interpret scripture exactly alike. Concerning Dispensational Theology, or End Times, there are almost as many varying interpretations as there are dates that have been set for Jesus to physically return.

➤ Whether Jesus will return in an earthly body and rapture the *church*...

➤ Or if the Second Coming happened on the Day of Pentecost...

➤ Or if the Second Coming of Christ is not meant to be relegated to a physical body and literal return at all, but rather is the Spirit of Christ returning and being shed abroad in the hearts of all humanity where *all men shall see Him together* and *the earth shall be filled with the glory of the Lord as the waters cover the sea?*

Whatever your specific theology may be, I declare with you that we all love *the APPEARING* of the Christ – however that might transpire!

As we begin to discuss *Dispensational Theology* or the ideas of *End Times* - allow me to warn you again of the dangers of literalism. *For the letter (or literal) kills, but the Spirit gives life.*

For example, scripture tells us that God *owns the cattle on a thousand hills.* Obviously there are more than one thousand hills with cattle in existence right now on the earth. So, does God only specifically own the cattle on one thousand of those hills? Or is this a figure that is representative of infinity or endlessness, suggesting to us that God owns everything? When we apply this logic to some of the dispensational timelines that have been created by men, we can understand that to take a metaphorical book, or to take symbolic prophecies, and from them manufacture exact timelines may lead us astray and into a fear consciousness.

When scripture says that *God keeps covenant to a thousand generations,* does this mean the one thousand and first generation is out of luck? When Jesus tells the disciples to *Forgive seventy times seven,* does this mean after four hundred and ninety times the disciple is no longer required to forgive?

The arrogance of man to think that he can exactly figure out an ultimately unknowable, unconquerable God! No flesh shall ever claim complete mastery of the mystery of Spirit.

THE LIKE – AS PRINCIPLE

What we find often times in scripture is the LIKE-AS principle. This is LIKE that or this is AS that. Words such as LIKE and AS point us toward the metaphorical nature of truth and the need to rethink literal interpretations and applications of scripture. After all, Jesus taught in the LIKE-AS principle (as He taught in parable, metaphor or allegory).

For a thousand years in thy sight are but AS yesterday when it is past, and AS a watch in the night.
Psalm 90:4 – KJV

But do not forget this one thing, dear friends: With the Lord a day is LIKE a thousand years, and a thousand years are LIKE a day.
II Peter 3:8 NIV

Your enemy the devil prowls around LIKE a roaring lion looking for someone to devour.
I Peter 5:8 – NIV

There is no literal or mathematical equation rendering to us the answer that one 24 hour day of God is the exact equivalent of 1000 years to man. Notice the word *LIKE! A day is LIKE a thousand years.* This simply means that our version of time cannot be compared to God's vision of time. Remember, we live in *time* while God exists in eternity or in *timelessness.*

It is this LIKE – AS principle which leads us to some very significant questions when speaking of End Times:

➢ **Is the book of Revelation to be taken literally or metaphorically?**

➢ Is there a literal *millennial period* (or one thousand year season) where we, the righteous will have been *raptured* into Heaven and then return to earth to live among those who have survived *the Tribulation*?

➢ Is there a literal group of *one hundred and forty four thousand virgins* who go to Heaven while the other *lesser* righteous people are left to go through the tribulation and Armageddon (Revelation 14)?

➢ During *Armageddon* will the blood of this battle actually reach the *bridle of the horse* (Revelation 14)? There is not enough blood on the earth (even if every living thing was slaughtered) to cover the earth five or six feet high in blood.

➢ Are there literally two separate dragons that will come out of the sea, or are these dragons depicting the world systems that do not recognize the providence of God (Revelation 12, 13, 16 and 20)?

These questions are designed to cause us to seek a deeper understanding around the ideas of End Times. Interestingly enough, the word *Apocalypse* (thought by some to mean *the end of the world*) actually means *the revealing of hidden truth*. Perhaps the Apocalypse is not the end of the world at all, but only the end of an Age where the truth has been hidden from us.

DANGER IN LITERALISM (THE ANTICHRIST)

Whatever your take on End Times theology may be, let us be aware of some of the dangers surrounding literal interpretations. Literalism draws us into the confinement of black and white or concrete thinking which does not allow room for growth, progress or flexibility. And, anything that is incapable of bending will eventually be broken. Furthermore, literalism is to be credited with the separation, segregation and violence that has and does exist between many religions and people groups.

Is the antichrist a literal person?
Or a spirit?
Or simply a state of consciousness?

but every spirit that does not acknowledge Jesus is not from God. This is the SPIRIT OF THE ANTICHRIST, which you have heard is coming and even now is ALREADY IN THE WORLD.
I John 4:3 - NIV

Notice this passage refers to the antichrist, not as a person, but as a *SPIRIT* – a spirit that thinks a certain way which is simply describing to us a state of consciousness. Furthermore, we see that the antichrist is not coming, but is *ALREADY IN THE WORLD*. The danger in believing that the antichrist is a literal person, and not a spirit, is that at some point, someone will accuse someone of being the antichrist. This assigning of personage to the antichrist becomes especially dangerous when a maniacal religious zealot like Adolf Hitler expands this assignation to an entire group such as he did to the Jewish people. If we believe the antichrist is a literal person human nature will drive us to find him and then rid the world of him. This, however, is the same type of literal thinking and religious fanaticism that sent planes into the World Trade Center.

Will a specific person actually bear the mark of the beast – 666 – on his head? Or is this dealing with a mindset that does not recognize the Christ? Again, the danger of the literal mind is that when it perceives that the antichrist is a literal person (or group of people) – at some point it will try to identify this person…and already has.

I John 2, I John 4 and II John 1 all speak of the antichrist as a spirit or as a spirit with a person(s) that denies Jesus became the Christ. We can clearly see that this spirit already exists in the world. With regards to an Inclusive Perspective – the religious mind that denies the world is reconciled to God through Christ may be unconsciously operating in an antichrist mentality.

SETTING DATES

Another danger in interpreting scripture literally around the ideas of End Times is the practice of setting dates for Christ's return. Christ is, and has always been in the earth. Dates have been set since the time of the Apostle Paul who was so convinced of the imminent and immediate return of Christ that he instructed his single disciples not to marry *(I Corinthians 7:25-31)*.

Concerning End Times, it is important not only to know what you believe, but why you believe it and to know the actual origin of concepts people are trying to teach you. The scripture in Thessalonians that refers to us being *caught up in the clouds* has for many years been used as the foundational evidence for the Rapture Theory. The truth is, the word *rapture* is not even in the Bible.

This particular, and may I say peculiar, dispensational teaching was popularized by a man named John Neslon Darby in the 1800's. Some of the teaching was based on scripture and some was conjecture surrounding a very graphic but momentary vision a little girl had at an emotional altar call to which she responded during a tent revival. An entire doctrine was built on and around the information shared by Margaret McDonald, and many, still to this day, adopt it as sacred even though it is solidly supported nowhere in scripture.

Setting dates for when Christ will return causes a stagnation of purpose and an interruption of mission. What is the mission? To help make the *earth the footstool* of God once again! When we sit waiting, gazing into the sky, there is a tendency to become too heavenly minded that we are no earthly good.

There is also a danger of teaching a literal return of Christ and a subsequent rapture. If we are waiting to be taken out of the earth, why would we care for the earth right now? Dispensational thinking promotes the ideas that we are merely strangers and foreigners just "passing through" this earth – and that this earth is "not our home."

When we adopt these ideals, the care for our planet and for those inhabiting the earth will eventually and inevitably be neglected. The problem that results, and that has evolved, around this type of literal interpretation is that this sort of literal mentality develops a separatist (or pharisaical) mentality and encourages a departure from a social conscience.

But when we shift from the idea that "the earth is not my home" to the idea that "the earth is the Lord's" then suddenly we become more conscious of how we treat the earth. We think more about what shape we are leaving the earth in for our children. Is the earth a better place because we've been here? Did we leave the space we inhabited better or worse?

The earth is the LORD's, and everything in it, the world,
and all who live in it
Psalm 24:1 - NIV

The time has come for… destroying those who destroy the earth."
Revelation 11:18 - NIV

God does not have to destroy those who destroy (or neglect) the earth. Why? Those who are so rapture-minded, and who choose to neglect the earth, will eventually destroy themselves if they do not recognize that…

➢ the earth is the Lord's,

➢ everything in the earth is the Lord's,

➤ all who live in the earth are the Lord's.

You will hear of wars and rumors of wars, but SEE TO IT THAT YOU ARE NOT ALARMED. Such things must happen, but THE END IS STILL TO COME.
Matthew 24:6 - NIV

When you hear of wars and rumors of wars, DO NOT BE ALARMED. Such things must happen, but THE END IS STILL TO COME.
Mark 13:7 – NIV

Wars and rumors of wars have always been (and as long as the literal religious mind is alive there will always be war between religions and nations rising against other nations). Mankind has been at war with itself for as long as we have had some type of a recorded history.

Nation will rise against nation, and kingdom against kingdom. There will be famines and earthquakes in various places.
Matthew 24:7 - NIV

Earthquakes and famine have always been.

I watched as he opened the sixth seal. There was a great earthquake. The sun turned black like sackcloth made of goat hair, the whole moon turned blood red
Revelation 6:12 – NIV (also Joel 2:31 Acts 2:20)

The *moon turned to blood* or turned red during the last lunar eclipse.

The *sun was darkened* during the last solar eclipse.

Israel seems to perpetually be in conflict and has been so always, even *before* the birth of Jesus.

So, how will we know when the end is near?

> *And this GOSPEL OF THE KINGDOM will be preached*
> *in all the world as a WITNESS to all the nations,*
> *and THEN THE END WILL COME.*
> **Matthew 24:14 - NKJV**

The Gospel of the Kingdom must be preached to the world. And, preaching the Gospel of the Kingdom is not necessarily preaching the person of Jesus. The Gospel of the Kingdom is the message Jesus preached while He was here. So, the end does not come when we preach Jesus to the whole world, but when we preach the message and principles of Jesus to the world. This is how you preach the Gospel of the Kingdom *as a witness*. When personage is promoted above principle, we remain trapped in culture and tribe mentality and are still estranged from the strategy of preaching the Kingdom as a *witness* to all nations. Principles will bear *witness* with someone when personage may not.

The year 2012 has been predicted and prophesied by many cultures as the literal end of the world. 2012 is actually the end of the age: the Age of Pisces. The zodiac symbol associated with Jesus is the Pisces fish (or the Jesus fish). Jesus, the Person, comes to introduce us to Christ, the Spirit. Now, as the Age of Pisces is ending, the Age of Aquarius is dawning. And, Aquarius (aqua, aquarium) symbolizes water. So, 2012 is the end of the world as we know it. Religious division and the hostility caused by promoting only one savior figure, or one holy book over another, will come to an end.

And, there will be a new spiritual understanding that we are all the children and image of God!

THE GOSPEL OF THE KINGDOM

What is the Gospel of the Kingdom? Again, preaching the Gospel of the Kingdom is not preaching the person of Jesus but the principles of Jesus. The Gospel of the Kingdom is simply a way of thinking, living and loving. Many different scriptures reveal to us what the Gospel of the Kingdom is, but when we read the 5th chapter of Matthew we see a clear and concise description. Here are the highlights of the most famous sermon ever delivered in history (The Sermon on the Mount):

-v. 5, 7 and 9 - *Be meek; be merciful; and be a peacemaker.*

-v. 13-15 - *Season your environment and shine light into darkness.*

-v. 38-48 - *Return good for evil – and bless and pray for your enemies.*

-v. 6 - *Continue to hunger and thirst for God – and you will be filled.*

-v. 8, 21-22, 27-28 - *And, know that when your heart is pure - you will not require a law to be justified or to show you how to love God and prefer your fellow man.*

We can easily see from this that the Kingdom of God is not a set of rules to be followed. But, the Kingdom of God is a consciousness to seek after.

For the kingdom of God is not a matter of eating and drinking, but of righteousness, peace and joy in the Holy Spirit
Romans 14:7 - NIV

Furthermore, when this Gospel of the Kingdom is preached to all the world *as a witness*, this is not the *end* of the *world,* but rather the *end* of the *age.* This marks the beginning of a new way, a new thought, a new era. Consider the words of Jesus regarding the End of an age...

The Law and the Prophets were proclaimed until John. Since that time, the good news of the kingdom of God is being preached, and everyone is forcing his way into it.
Luke 16:16 - NIV

The age of the law and the prophets was coming to an end as Jesus introduced the Gospel of the Kingdom. Yet, even when one age ends, it continues to try to sneak its way into the next age. Remember, *the Law and the Prophets were until John* – but now we have come to the Kingdom Age.

About eight days after Jesus said this, he took Peter, John and James with him and went up onto a mountain to pray. As he was praying, the appearance of his face changed, and his clothes became as bright as a flash of lightning. Two men, MOSES (the Law) and ELIJAH (the Prophets), appeared in glorious splendor, talking with Jesus. They spoke about his departure, which he was about to bring to fulfillment at Jerusalem. Peter and his companions were very sleepy, but when they became fully awake, they saw his glory and the two men standing with him. As the men were leaving Jesus, Peter said to him, "Master, it is good for us to be here. Let us put up three shelters (or altars)—one for you, one for Moses and one for Elijah."
(He did not know what he was saying.)
While he was speaking, a cloud appeared and enveloped them, and they were afraid as they entered the cloud. A voice came from the cloud, saying, "THIS IS MY SON, WHOM I HAVE CHOSEN; LISTEN TO HIM." When the voice had spoken, they found that

JESUS WAS ALONE (without Moses and Elijah). The disciples kept this to themselves, and told no one at that time what they had seen.
Luke 9:28-36 NIV

Notice that the same disciple (Peter) who had the revelation of the Christ has now made the suggestion to build altars to Moses and to Elijah. Jesus does not respond but the Father does. How? God sends a cloud to surround all of them, then speaks to the disciples that they should now listen only to Jesus. And when the cloud disappears Jesus is standing alone, without Moses and Elijah. The preaching and teaching of the law, the prophets or even of the Jesus person will not mark the end of the age. It is the preaching of the Gospel of the Kingdom that will usher us into the next age.

Yes, we live in a difficult time replete with its own challenges (and opportunities). However, let us not sensationalize events that have always been constantly occurring in an attempt to prove the validity of a theory or in an effort to defend a theology. Therefore, let us set our intention, and focus our attention, on communicating and demonstrating the Good News of the Kingdom to every living creature.

JESUS ALREADY RETURNED ~ AT PENTECOST

Behold, I am coming QUICKLY.
Revelation 3:11; 22:7; 22:12, 20 - NKJV

When the Bible continually says that Jesus is coming *quickly,* what exactly does this mean? Does quickly mean two thousand years later? Have we been stood up for our date with Jesus? If you are a literalist you might be able to rationalize this *not so quick return* of Jesus by using the *one day is LIKE a thousand with God* excuse. And, by using this interpretation we have only waited two days for Jesus to return. As we wrestle with this question (Why is it taking so long for Jesus to return if He said He was coming quickly?) consider these verses in John.

"But now I go away to Him who sent Me, and none of you asks Me, 'Where are You going?' But because I have said these things to you, sorrow has filled your heart. Nevertheless I tell you the truth. IT IS TO YOUR ADVANTAGE THAT I GO AWAY; FOR IF I DO NOT GO AWAY, THE HELPER WILL NOT COME TO YOU; BUT IF I DEPART, I WILL SEND HIM TO YOU."
John 16:5-7 NKJV

"A LITTLE WHILE, and you will not see Me; and again a LITTLE WHILE, and you will see Me, because I go to the Father." Then some of His disciples said among themselves, "What is this that He says to us, 'A little while, and you will not see Me; and again a little while, and you will see Me'; and, 'because I go to the Father'?"
John 16:16-17 NKJV

Notice several key points from these two passages in the 16th chapter of John:

> Jesus prophesies that He is going away (but only for a little while).

> He then adds that it is *to our advantage* that He go away. Why? What would be the advantage of Jesus going away?

> Jesus promises that He is going to send to us the Holy Spirit.

Allow me to offer you an interesting thought. Jesus said that He was leaving and then that He would be returning quickly. And, He did! Jesus returned at Pentecost forty days after He ascended. The Spirit that fell on those gathered in the Upper Room was Jesus returning just as He had promised.

If Pentecost was indeed the Second Coming of Christ, why are we still waiting for Him to return in bodily form? Many Evangelical Christians take issue with the fact that Jewish people do not accept the divinity of Jesus. These Christians find it hard to understand why the Jews are still waiting for the Messiah since they (Christians) believe Jesus to be the fulfillment of the Jewish Messianic Prophecy. Yet these same Christians, who have access to the book of Acts that clearly indicates that Jesus returned at Pentecost in Spirit form, still wait on a physical *Second Coming*. Is this not just a different form of denying Christ, the exact thing they accuse the Jews of doing?

> Jesus left as a Man – and returned as a Spirit.

> Jesus ascended as a Character – and descended as a Consciousness.

> Jesus went away as a Person – and came back as a Presence.

In II Corinthians we can clearly see this transition and transformation from knowing Jesus as flesh to knowing Christ as Spirit.

For we know that if our earthly house, this tent, is destroyed, we have a building from God, a house not made with hands, eternal in the heavens. For in this we groan, earnestly desiring to be clothed with our habitation which is from heaven, if indeed, having been clothed, we shall not be found naked. For we who are in this tent groan, being burdened, not because we want to be unclothed, but further clothed, that mortality may be swallowed up by life. Now He who has prepared us for this very thing is God, who also has given us the Spirit as a guarantee... Therefore, from now on, we regard no one according to the flesh. EVEN THOUGH WE HAVE KNOWN CHRIST ACCORDING TO THE FLESH, YET WE KNOW HIM THUS NO LONGER. Therefore, if anyone is in Christ, he is a new creation; old things have passed away; behold, all things have become new.
II Corinthians 5:1-5, 16-17 NKJV

➢ Our bodies are a temporary dwelling (or a *tent*).

➢ Similarly, the *body* of Jesus was only a temporary dwelling for Him.

➢ But we also have an eternal house that is not fleshly (or *not made with hands*). And, we groan and yearn to be *furthered clothed* – we long for that eternal habitation.

➢ Likewise, the *body* of Jesus desired to be clothed with Eternal Spirit.

➢ *Mortality will be swallowed up by Life* – or what is temporary will be overcome by what is permanent.

➢ The mortality of the Jesus Person has now been swallowed up by the immortality of the Christ Presence.

➢ Now, we have been prepared for this transition of the temporary flesh of Jesus to become eternal Christ Presence. And, the guarantee God gives us that this transformation is complete is the Holy Spirit.

➢ In other words, the Presence of the Holy Ghost at Pentecost was the guarantee that this transformation had been completed, that Jesus had become Spirit. And further, now that Jesus has shown us the way, we can become Spirit as well. Jesus is *the firstborn...among MANY brethren!*

➢ Yes, all of us have known Christ *ACCORDING TO THE FLESH* (first the natural, then the spiritual).

➢ However, we no longer know Christ according to the flesh (and Jesus, is Christ according to the flesh).

➢ The Holy Spirit; Holy Ghost; Presence of God is the new, the now and the eternal expression of what we knew as the temporary flesh called Jesus.

The question for us now is this, "Are we *in Christ*?" We know by now that *Christ IS ALL, and is IN ALL (Colossians 3)*. However, even though Christ is IN ALL doesn't necessarily mean that all are IN CHRIST. In other words, some are still connected only to the Jesus Person and have not yet walked into the Christ Consciousness. But, IF we are IN CHRIST we are *a new creation, old things have passed away and all things are made new;* even our perceptions about the Jesus Person and our paradigms about the eternal Christ Presence all become new.

Once we truly begin to know Christ by the Spirit we will effectively open a portal that will eventually and inevitably transport us to the knowledge of ourselves and others as Spirit.

SPECIALNESS

In my humble opinion, the greatest danger in literal interpretations of End Times is the creation and enabling of SPECIALNESS. The ideas surrounding End Times theology boldly and unashamedly promote ISRAEL as the literal center of the universe, and the people of Israel as the *most* special people of God.

This type of theology prophesies conflict and then manifests it.

> ➢ When there is a CHOSEN, by default there is an UNCHOSEN.

> ➢ When there is a CALLED, there is an UNCALLED.

> ➢ When there is a FAVORITE, there is a LESS FAVORED.

> ➢ When there is a SPECIAL PEOPLE, then there are LESS SPECIAL PEOPLE.

Exclusive promotion of Israel is destructive. No one chooses where or to whom they are born. Thus, people should not be judged less or more special on the basis of a criterion beyond their control, and therefore cannot be deemed special simply by virtue of their birth. But these are the conditions that we as Bible-believing Christians have created and promoted concerning the physical nation of Israel. The Evangelical mindset will protect a nation and religion that does not accept or acknowledge Christ (Judaism) while simultaneously rejecting another religion (Islam) seemingly for the very same offense. There is no way this is anything other than prejudice. It is possible to love Israel and the Jewish people without affording them special treatment based solely on the fact that we perceive them to be more special to God than Palestinians, Jordanians, or Iraqis.

All we need do is follow the stories of Cain and Abel; Esau (bearer of the birthright and special blessing) and Jacob (the one who deceived his brother out of the birthright and blessing); Joseph (the favorite) and his brothers (those who were embittered by their father's showing favoritism) in order to comprehend the inherent dysfunction that fostering specialness produces.

Now, consider the specialness placed upon Isaac and the subsequent expulsion of Ishmael. Although both were his biological sons, because of specialness Abraham actually disowned Ishmael in favor of Isaac. Again, specialness prophesies conflict and then manifests it. The ongoing saga in the Middle East will never be solved as long as there is dispensational support for specialness. In the Christ consciousness, we all are now the *Spiritual Israel* of God.

And the glory of the LORD will be revealed, and all mankind together will see it. For the mouth of the LORD has spoken.
Isaiah 40:5 - NIV

Then I, John, saw the holy city, New Jerusalem, coming down out of heaven from God, prepared as a bride adorned for her husband. And I heard a loud voice from heaven saying, "Behold, the tabernacle of God is with men, and He will dwell with them, and they shall be His people. God Himself will be with them and be their God." But I saw no temple in it, for the Lord God Almighty and the Lamb are its temple.
Revelation 21:2-3, 22 NKJV

Notice in this passage the lack of literalism in the New Jerusalem:

➢ There are no literal temples because the Presence of God will become the temple.

> ➤ There are no literal tabernacles as the tabernacle will become just that, the habitation of God and humanity together.

If Jesus is to return specifically to Israel as a person in a fleshly body, how would it be possible for *all of mankind see this together?* Personage is limited to place and space. But, Presence has no limitations. Jesus, the Person and Israel, the place must now make room for Christ, the Presence.

Why do we continue to try to put Jesus back into a body? When He so obviously returned as a Spirit at Pentecost? That very well could have been the Second Coming He was talking about when He said *soon.* But even someone as enlightened as Paul can slip back into the literal mind. Paul believed Jesus when He said He would return *soon,* so much so that he instructed some of his followers to not even take the time to marry. But why didn't his enlightenment kick in when the Day of Pentecost arrived? Why didn't he say, "Here it is. Christ (the Spirit of Christ) has returned in the form of a dove. He has brought men together. He showed up in all of us."

The Holy Bible of Inclusion

Part VII - JESUS and THE CHRIST

---◆---

-NO MAN comes to the Father EXCEPT THROUGH ME-
(Is Gandhi in Hell?)

✱

-NO OTHER NAME…but The NAME of JESUS-

✱

-Thou art THE CHRIST-

✱

-CHRIST "IS" BEFORE JESUS "WAS"-

✱

-AWAKENING THE CHRIST WITHIN JESUS-

✱

-Why do you CALL ME GOOD?-

✱

-AVATARS AND OTHER INCARNATIONS OF THE
CHRIST-

✱

-THE MYSTERY OF MELCHIZEDEK "the CHRIST"-

✱

-I CAN'T BE JESUS…BUT I CAN BECOME THE CHRIST-

✱

NO MAN COMES TO THE FATHER EXCEPT THROUGH ME

Why is it necessary to differentiate between Jesus of Nazareth and the Christ Spirit? Between the Jesus *Person* and the Christ *Principle*? Is there even a difference?   *Jesus*, and *the Christ*, are the same, yet different, simultaneously.   How can this be?   The similarities are overwhelming, awe-inspiring and worthy of our recognition and reverence. Yet, there are a few differences – also worth noting, and necessary to mention, in order for us to individually and collectively achieve a deeper revelation of Inclusion and a more powerful expression of Oneness.

The reason I will go to great lengths *scripturally* to show this significant difference between Jesus and the Christ is because so many preach and promote the idea that a majority of God's creation will be kept out of heaven (and banished to hell) because they may not come to God through the Jesus *Person* - although myriad people of other religions desperately love God and sincerely connect to the *Christ Spirit* through their worship.

> *Jesus said to him, "I am the way, the truth, and the life.*
> *NO ONE COMES TO THE FATHER except through Me.*
> ***John 14:6 - NKJV***

When Jesus says, *No one comes to the Father except through Me* does this mean no one comes to God except through the *Historical, Physical Person of Jesus of Nazareth?*   Or does this mean that in order to be set free from the lower human consciousness (or animalistic nature) creation must connect to the *Eternal Spiritual Principle of the Christ?* What is the difference between the Jesus *Person* and the Christ *Principle*?

As we struggle through this moment of philosophical bewilderment and press our way beyond the theological angst of seeing both the disparities and the similarities between Jesus and the Christ, allow me to pose a very tough question with which we must wrestle:

IS MOHATMA GANDHI IN HELL?

Is the man who inspired Martin Luther King, Jr., and the Civil Rights movement in America, in hell, being tormented and tortured for all eternity? Gandhi was not a Christian and did not come to God through the *Name* of Jesus. But, did Gandhi carry the Christ Spirit within (even though he did not receive the Jesus Person as his *personal Lord and Savior* nor ever say the *magical prayer* - that we know of)?

If we say that Gandhi was not in touch with the Christ Spirit, then what Spirit was it that miraculously guided him to use the strategy of *love* to end the killing and brutality in India? What Spirit inspired this movement of love that ultimately defeated hatred? And, what Spirit in Gandhi connected with Martin Luther King, Jr.? If Gandhi lived in *darkness* what fellowship should the *light* in King have had with the supposed *darkness* in Gandhi?

It is interesting to note that Gandhi loved and revered Jesus of Nazareth. He read the Gospels often and encouraged Hindus everywhere to follow Jesus' teaching on the *Kingdom of God,* adding that if Hindus would follow this teaching that they would find their way to enlightenment, nirvana and gain access to heaven. Once he was asked by the Christian missionary, E. Stanley Jones, *"Mr. Gandhi, though you quote the words of Christ often, why is it that you appear to so adamantly reject becoming His follower?"* Gandhi answered, *"Oh. I don't reject your Christ. I love your Christ. It's just that so many of your Christians are so unlike your Christ."*

Gandhi loved Christ and to a degree, followed His teaching, but he never actually became or took on the title of being, a "born-again" Christian. He once remarked, *"I do not like Christians. I would have become a Christian were it not for Christians."* Gandhi connected to the Christ within Jesus, but not to the religion, or the misinterpretations created in and around the name of Jesus. Gandhi seemed to be able to maintain a powerful connection with God without promoting the necessity of connecting to God through any one particular religion or religious / Christ figure. Thus, he once famously said, *"God has no religion...I believe in the fundamental Truths in all the great religions of the world. I believe they are all God-given. I came to the conclusion long ago...that all religions were true and also that all had some error in them."*

Does religion, any religion, make an *error* by insisting that its particular way, or specific Savior character, is the only way to God?

This troubling query leads us to another imperative question raised about *Name*. Consider this scripture in the book of Acts.

Let it be known to you all, and to all the people of Israel, that by the name of Jesus Christ of Nazareth, whom you crucified, whom God raised from the dead, by Him this man stands here before you whole. This is the 'stone which was rejected by you builders, which has become the chief cornerstone.' Nor is there salvation in any other, for there is NO OTHER NAME under heaven given among men by which we must be saved.
Acts 4:10-12 NKJV

> ➤ Can someone connect to the *Nature* of the Universal Christ without confessing the *Name* of Jesus of Nazareth?

> ➤ Are we saved by simply the *Name* of Jesus – or by emulating the *Nature* of the Christ?

> ➢ Aren't there countless Christians who confess the *Name* of Jesus who in their daily lives exhibit absolutely no understanding, nor application, of the *Nature* and character of the Christ?

> ➢ Are we to believe that these Christians are saved solely by the *Name* of Jesus when they make little or no attempt to live out His most cherished principles while Gandhi remains damned for all eternity for being connected to God, not by the *Name* of the Jesus Person, but by connecting to God through and demonstrating in his own life the *Nature* of the Christ Principle?

While pondering this question (*Can someone connect to God without first connecting to Jesus of Nazareth?*) consider this quote by Howard Thurman taken from his timeless work *Jesus and the Disinherited*. Historical accounts tell us that Dr. Martin Luther King, Jr. actually carried a copy of this book with him on his many speaking engagements, journeys and marches. Howard Thurman served as a mentor to Dr. Martin Luther King, Jr.

To some God and Jesus may appeal in a way other than to us: some may come to faith in God and to love, without a conscious attachment to Jesus. Both nature and good men besides Jesus may lead us to God. They who seek God with all their hearts must, however, someday on their way meet Jesus.
Howard Thurman – Jesus and the Disinherited

Gandhi was obviously such a man, as described here by Thurman, who possessed a genuine connection with God, and to the Christ Spirit, without having an initial conscious attachment to Jesus. However, because Gandhi was a man who sought God with his whole heart and because he worshiped God in Spirit and in Truth, he eventually encountered and celebrated Jesus of Nazareth, although he never accepted the concept that Jesus was the *only way* to God.

NO OTHER NAME…BUT THE NAME OF JESUS

The name Jesus, in English, is simply *Joshua* (Yeshua in Hebrew). How many people would object if some Sunday morning their pastor stood in the pulpit and stated, "There is no other name than *Joshua* by which we can be saved?" Is the significance really in the *Name*? Or is it in the *Nature*? And is Jesus of Nazareth the only person in history who carried the nature of God and then gave His life for the salvation of others?

The NAME is Jesus.

But, the NATURE is the Christ.

Are we saved by the name of Joshua (Yeshua, Jesus)? Are we saved by the name *Joshua Christ (or Yeshua Christos)?* Or are we saved by the WAY that Jesus came to show us? Is *Christ* Jesus' last name? I say no, it is not. We don't know Jesus' last name. He was simply referred to as Jesus, or Joshua, of Nazareth. Christ is not part of Jesus' name but rather the *title* that Jesus carried.

Consider these thought provoking truths:

> ➢ The name *Christ* comes from the Greek word 'Christos' meaning *the anointed one.*

> ➢ The Hindu Savior character and Lord named *Krishna* has the same exact meaning as Christ. In the Greek it is also translated as *Christos*. A colloquial Bengali rendering of Krishna is *Kristo,* which is the same as the Spanish for Christ — *Cristo.*

> ➢ Christ, or Krishna, are more than just *names* – they are symbolic of the *Anointed* and *Divine Nature*.

> Similarly, Siddhartha Gautama was the name of the person who carried the title of *the Buddha*. Buddha is not the last name of Siddhartha Gautama anymore than Christ is the last name of Jesus of Nazareth. Buddha is the title of the "Enlightened One" that Siddhartha Gautama carried.

My family has become very close with a beautiful family from India who happen to be Hindu by religion. Several times a year, the living patriarch of their family, *Krishna*, comes to stay with the family for several months to see his children and to spend time with his grandchildren. He is one of the most peaceful and loving human beings I have ever encountered. As he and I were talking a few years ago he said to me, "When I was a little boy in India, Christian missionaries came to convert the Hindus into Christians. The missionaries soon became very frustrated because the Hindus were not converting. What these missionaries did not know is that *the Christ* has always been in India." He then went on to say, "My name, Krishna, in English is Christ-na."

I have to admit, as I have walked and talked and communed with this precious spirit, housed in a small Indian body that strangely enough, closely resembles Mohandas K. Gandhi, I have sensed more of the Presence of the Christ than while talking to many and in actuality, most of my fellow Christians.

THOU ART THE CHRIST

*When Jesus came into the coasts of Caesarea Philippi, he asked his
disciples, saying, Whom do men say that I the Son of man am? And
they said, Some say that thou art John the Baptist: some, Elias;
and others, Jeremias, or one of the prophets. He saith unto them,
But whom say ye that I am? And Simon Peter answered and said,
THOU ART THE CHRIST, the Son of the living God. And Jesus
answered and said unto him, Blessed art thou, Simon Barjona:
for FLESH AND BLOOD hath not revealed it unto thee, but my
FATHER WHICH IS IN HEAVEN. And I say also unto thee, That
thou art Peter, and upon this rock I will build my church;
and the gates of hell shall not prevail against it.*
Matthew 16:13-18 KJV

Remember that Peter already knew Jesus of Nazareth. Actually,
Peter and his brother James, had decided to forsake all and follow
Jesus more than twelve chapters earlier in the Gospel of Matthew.
By the sixteenth chapter of Matthew, they had eaten together and
fished together and walked together. But, all of the sudden, Peter (or
Simon) receives a revelation of *THE CHRIST*. Peter was familiar
with the *FLESH and BLOOD*, or the *Person* of Jesus. However,
flesh and blood, or an earthly, fleshly knowledge and attachment to
Jesus, will not necessarily reveal the Christ. The revelation of the
Christ is a heavenly, spiritual revelation.

Follow this way of seeing the differences between Flesh and Spirit:

Jesus = the Son of Man
Christ = the Son of God

Jesus = the Man of History
Christ = the Man of Mystery

Peter, and the other disciples knew Jesus of Nazareth. They had come to love and appreciate the Son of Man. However, they had not yet encountered (in consciousness) the Son of God. They were acquainted with Jesus by a human, *flesh and blood* interaction. The disciples knew the Man of History. Yet, they were ignorant of the Man of Mystery, *THE ETERNAL CHRIST*. They knew *CHRIST ACCORDING TO THE FLESH* (or Jesus of Nazareth) but now they have received a heavenly revelation of *the Christ!*

Even though we have known CHRIST ACCORDING TO THE
FLESH, yet now we know Him thus no longer.
II Corinthians 5:16 NKJV

Most Christians have a knowledge of *Christ according to the flesh* – or *Jesus*. Yet, after this section of researching the deeper biblical revelations of the Christ, my prayer is that you *know Him thus (according to the flesh) no longer!*

CHRIST "IS" BEFORE JESUS "WAS"

The mission of Jesus of Nazareth is to connect, or better to *reconnect* us, to the Christ. The Christ has always been in the world, even before Jesus was born. Consider this passage in Corinthians revealing to us that the Christ was present in the earth many years before Jesus was born in Bethlehem.

Moreover, brethren, I would not that ye should be ignorant, how that all our fathers were under the cloud, and all passed through the sea; And were all baptized unto Moses in the cloud and in the sea; And did all eat the same spiritual meat; And did all drink the same spiritual drink: for they drank of that spiritual Rock that followed them: and that Rock was Christ.
I Corinthians 10:1-4 KJV

Notice, that Paul gives us the revelation that the Christ was in the wilderness with Moses and the Israelites. Fourteen hundred years before Jesus was born, the Christ was present in the earth.

Then Nebuchadnezzar the king was astonished, and rose up in haste, and spake, and said unto his counsellors, Did not we cast three men bound into the midst of the fire? They answered and said unto the king, True, O king. He answered and said, Lo, I see four men loose, walking in the midst of the fire, and they have no hurt; and THE FORM OF THE FOURTH IS LIKE THE SON OF GOD.
Daniel 3:24-25 KJV

The same Christ that was in the wilderness with Moses was also with the three Hebrew children in the fiery furnace six hundred years before the birth of Jesus. Notice that even King Nebuchadnezzar saw this eternal spirit and then describes it as looking like the Son of God.

There are two references to a priestly king named Melchizedek in the Old Testament (Genesis and Psalms). There are nine references to Melchizedek in Paul's epistle to the Hebrews. We will not go into depth regarding Melchizedek until we get to the section "The Mystery of Melchizedek." However, for the sake of showing that Christ was in the world before the birth of Jesus, allow me to give you a bit of background about Melchizedek. It is also important to note that *the Christ* mentioned in the wilderness, and the *Christ Presence* referred to in the fiery furnace are not specifically tied to a person, Jesus or otherwise. However, we will see with Melchizedek that a Christ figure arises to us from the Bible that is OTHER THAN Jesus of Nazareth. Meaning, that more than one person can, and has, carried the Spirit of the Christ.

We find in the seventh chapter of Hebrews that Melchizedek is called the *King of Righteousness*, and also referred to as the *King of Peace*. The book of Hebrews also informs us that Melchizedek is born of God or from heaven as he is *without father, without mother, without genealogy, having neither beginning of days nor end of life* (Alpha and Omega – sound familiar yet?). Finally, Hebrews gives us the most significant revelation that Melchizedek was *made like the Son of God.*

This Melchizedek king-priest-person was nothing less than a Christ figure – *other* than Jesus of Nazareth. Melchizedek *the Christ* even predates Moses, as he lived on the earth during the lifetime of Abraham. Not only was Christ in the earth before Jesus, the Christ Spirit was present *before Abraham was born.* And, like Melchizedek, the Christ has *no beginning or ending.* However, the Christ continuously incarnates into a fleshly form along the path of history *in the fullness of time* to reconnect humanity to God when needed. We'll get into that in a moment.

Jesus of Nazareth tapped into this timeless Christ Spirit, Christ Awareness, or Christ Consciousness perhaps more fully than any man who has ever walked this planet. As Jesus begins to understand the eternal existence of the Christ, and the Presence of the Christ within Himself, He reveals a portion of this knowledge to the Pharisees who have come to question Him.

"Your father Abraham rejoiced at the thought of seeing my day; he saw it and was glad." "You are not yet fifty years old," the Jews said to him, "and you have seen Abraham!" "I tell you the truth," Jesus answered, "BEFORE ABRAHAM WAS BORN, I AM!" At this, they picked up stones to stone him, but Jesus hid himself, slipping away from the temple grounds.
John 8:56-59 - NIV

AWAKENING THE CHRIST WITHIN JESUS

As we discussed at the beginning of this section, Jesus of Nazareth and the Christ, are the same, yet different, at the same time. Let me say it this way – Jesus possessed the potential to become the Christ and eventually did become the Christ.

Contemplate this passage in Hebrews:

Although he was a son, he LEARNED OBEDIENCE from what he suffered and, once MADE PERFECT, he BECAME the source of eternal salvation for all who obey him and was designated by God to be high priest in the ORDER OF MELCHIZEDEK.
Hebrews 5:8-10 NIV

Let us delve into the deep truths in this passage one by one:

➤ Jesus was a son, but He *LEARNED OBEDIENCE*… Jesus carried the potential of becoming the Christ, yet there was a process of learning that He had to agree with and surrender to so that the Christ hidden and resident within Him might be revealed to the world.

➤ Once *MADE PERFECT*, He *BECAME*… Paul makes it clear to us that Jesus went through a process of being perfected. Thus, He *became* the Christ.

➤ IN the *ORDER OF MELCHIZEDEK*… Jesus became a high priest in the same order and designation as Melchizedek. In other words, Jesus was the Second Person to reflect the nature of the Christ that was first seen in the person of Melchizedek.

There are several scriptural references to Jesus becoming the Christ. Consider this explanation of part of His childhood:

> *And the Child grew and became strong in spirit, filled with wisdom; and the grace of God was upon Him.*
> ***Luke 2:40 - NKJV***

The grace of God was upon Him, but once again He *BECAME* strong in spirit. Jesus *grew* in the knowledge of His potential.

> *I will proclaim the decree of the LORD: He said to me, "You are my Son; today I have BECOME your Father.*
> ***Psalm 2:7 - NIV***

Some may assume that the Son mentioned here in the 2nd Psalm is speaking of David. Actually, David is prophesying of the coming of Jesus (as we see in the book of Acts).

> *We tell you the good news: What God promised our fathers he has fulfilled for us, their children, by raising up Jesus. As it is written in the second Psalm: 'You are my Son; today I have BECOME your Father.*
> ***Acts 13:32-33 NIV***

Both in the Psalms and in Acts, God *BECAME* the Father of Jesus, *AFTER* the necessary process of perfection.

> *God, who at VARIOUS TIMES and in VARIOUS WAYS spoke in time past to the fathers by the prophets, has in these last days spoken to us by His Son, whom He has appointed heir of all things,*

through whom also He made the worlds; who being the brightness of His glory and the express image of His person, and upholding all things by the word of His power, when He had by Himself purged our sins, sat down at the right hand of the Majesty on high, having BECOME so much better than the angels, as He has by inheritance obtained a more excellent name than they.
For to which of the angels did He ever say: " You are My Son, TODAY I HAVE BEGOTTEN YOU." And again: " I will be to Him a Father, And He shall be to Me a Son."
Hebrews 1:1-5 NKJV

Let us dissect the truths in this first chapter of Hebrews:

> ➢ God (who sits in eternity) at *VARIOUS TIMES and WAYS* (spoke into time) by the prophets and has ALSO spoken through Jesus. Immediately we see the reference to God speaking through *many* messengers as well as through Jesus.

> ➢ Notice again, that Jesus *BECAME so much better than the angels* as He cooperated with the process of becoming the Christ, or surrendered to the Christ within Him.

> ➢ Finally, be aware that Jesus was both born as a begotten son and *became* a begotten son. Thus, *TODAY I have begotten You.*

Jesus carried the potential of becoming the Christ. Yet, there was a necessary process of uncovering the Christ within Him. In the next section we will look at an interaction between Jesus and a Canaanite woman that will serve as a very difficult example of the difference between Jesus and the Christ as we encounter an exclusive, and even somewhat racist Jesus of Nazareth.

WHY DO YOU CALL ME GOOD?

One of the greatest transformations in the history of mankind is that of Jesus of Nazareth becoming the Christ. Along His path to personal awakening, and to becoming the Savior of the world, there were several incidences we can study that reveal to us the slight, yet significant, differences between Jesus and the Christ.

> *A certain ruler asked him, "Good teacher, what must I do to inherit eternal life?" "WHY DO YOU CALL ME GOOD?" Jesus answered. "NO ONE IS GOOD—EXCEPT GOD ALONE."*
> **Luke 18:18-19 NIV (also Mark 10:18)**

> *When he came near the place where the road goes down the Mount of Olives, the whole crowd of disciples began joyfully to praise God in loud voices for all the miracles they had seen: "Blessed is the king who comes in the name of the Lord! Peace in heaven and glory in the highest!" Some of the Pharisees in the crowd said to Jesus, "Teacher, rebuke your disciples!" "I tell you," he replied, "IF THEY KEEP QUIET, THE STONES WILL CRY OUT."*
> **Luke 19:37-40 NIV**

What a transformation in consciousness! Jesus moved from rebuking a person for calling Him *good* – and teaching this certain ruler that *no one is good* but God – to telling the Pharisees that He is so worthy of worship that if the people *keep quiet* the very rocks, nature itself, would begin to *cry out* praises to Him. The question is this - What happened between the 18ᵗʰ and 19ᵗʰ chapter of Luke? Obviously some type of awakening or enlightenment occurred in Jesus. What was taking place? Jesus of Nazareth was becoming the Christ!

This instance of Jesus growing out of His humanity and into His Divinity is a relatively painless story, perhaps even pleasant, for most Christians. However, the next example may be a bit harder for us to swallow. Especially if we are more tightly tied to the Jesus Person than to the Christ Principle.

Leaving that place, Jesus withdrew to the region of Tyre and Sidon. A Canaanite woman from that vicinity came to him, crying out, "Lord, Son of David, have mercy on me! My daughter is suffering terribly from demon-possession." Jesus did not answer a word. So his disciples came to him and urged him, "Send her away, for she keeps crying out after us." He answered, "I was sent ONLY TO THE LOST SHEEP OF ISRAEL." The woman came and knelt before him. "Lord, help me!" she said. He replied, "It is not right to take the children's bread and toss it to THEIR DOGS." "Yes, Lord," she said, "but even the dogs eat the crumbs that fall from their masters' table." Then Jesus answered, "Woman, you have great faith! Your request is granted." And her daughter was healed from that very hour.
Matthew 15:21-28 NIV (also Mark 7:24-30)

Notice the limited consciousness, and concern, that Jesus has at this time regarding anyone outside of His specific circle, class or culture. After openly ignoring this Canaanite woman He then openly rejects her and her kind saying to her,

I was sent ONLY to the lost sheep of ISRAEL.

But the woman is too desperate to be offended. She begs of Jesus again. This time He responds to her by calling her a name (perhaps even some sort of racial slur).

It is not right to take the CHILDREN'S (Hebrews, Israelites) bread and toss it to THE DOGS (anyone who is not Israeli or of Hebrew descent).

Finally, that which was holy in this woman (the Christ) touches that which was holy in Jesus (the Christ). Let me say it this way, after wading through the humiliation of being ignored, rejected and called a name, the Christ Spirit which was resident within this woman wakes up the *Providential Christ Principle* inside of Jesus which was lying dormant inside of, and being hidden by, the *Provincial Jesus Person.*

This is a good place to ask the questions once again:

> ➢ Are we saved by the Jesus Person?
> ➢ Or by the Christ Principle?

> ➢ Are we saved by saying the Name of Jesus?
> ➢ Or by connecting to the Nature of the Christ?

In the 4th Chapter of John we find a Jesus who is more inclusive in His perspective and desire to reach those outside of his culture, and those outside of His specific religion. What we are encountering here is not so much the Jesus Person as it is the Christ Principle *within* the Jesus Person. He has widened the scope of His earthly ministry from exclusively being designated to the *lost sheep of Israel* to understanding that His ministry was to the whole world! Notice that Jesus has grown out of His religiously, racially and culturally driven limitations, and now understands that He *had to go* through Samaria – a place that Jews almost never frequented (as Jews and Samaritans had no dealings with each other).

Therefore, when the Lord knew that the Pharisees had heard that Jesus made and baptized more disciples than John (though Jesus Himself did not baptize, but His disciples), He left Judea and departed again to Galilee. BUT HE NEEDED TO GO THROUGH SAMARIA.
John 4:1-4 - NKJV

And many of the Samaritans of that city believed in Him because of the word of the woman who testified, "He told me all that I ever did." So when the Samaritans had come to Him, they urged Him to stay with them; and He stayed there two days. And many more believed because of His own word. Then they said to the woman, "Now we believe, not because of what you said, for we ourselves have heard Him and we know that this is indeed THE CHRIST, THE SAVIOR OF THE WORLD."
John 4:39-42 - NKJV

...From Jesus, provincial leader of the *lost sheep of Israel*...to the Christ, Providential *Savior of the World*. If Jesus grew in grace and in truth, we will and must follow His example! Jesus is our Way-maker; our Way-shower; our Elder Brother. Jesus becomes for us *the firstborn among MANY brethren!* There is a Christ within us all just waiting to be recovered, discovered and uncovered.

"Sir," the woman said, "I can see that you are a prophet. Our fathers worshiped on this mountain, but YOU JEWS CLAIM THAT THE PLACE WHERE WE MUST WORSHIP IS IN JERUSALEM." Jesus declared, "Believe me, woman, a time is coming when you will worship the Father NEITHER ON THIS MOUNTAIN NOR IN JERUSALEM...Yet a time is coming and has now come when the true worshipers will worship the Father in spirit and truth, for they

are the kind of worshipers the Father seeks. God is SPIRIT, and his worshipers must worship in spirit and in truth."
John 4:19-24 NIV

Also, notice in this 4th chapter of John that Jesus, during this conversation with a Samaritan woman, does not promote the idea of converting her to His familiar type, or place, of worship. Interesting to note that He, in essence, tells her, "I don't want you dragging Me to your mountain, and I won't drag you back to Jerusalem." But rather, Jesus encourages her to contemplate the thought that...

- ➢ *GOD IS SPIRIT*, not flesh;

- ➢ *GOD IS SPIRITUAL*, not religious;

- ➢ *GOD IS PRINCIPLE*, not a person;

- ➢ *GOD IS NATURE*, not a name;

- ➢ *GOD IS CONSCIOUSNESS*, not a character.

Jesus, the Son of Man and the Flesh Person would have either ignored or rejected this woman, or better still, would have tried to drag her back to Jerusalem, converting her to His religion.

Christ, the Son of God and Universal Principle – understands that it doesn't matter whether you worship God on a mountain or in Jerusalem – or whether you connect to God by the Name of Jesus or by the Nature of the Christ.

AVATARS AND OTHER INCARNATIONS OF THE CHRIST

As we swim out into some very deep waters (concerning the difference between Jesus and the Christ) consider this passage from the 1st chapter of Hebrews:

God, who at VARIOUS TIMES and in VARIOUS WAYS spoke in time past to the fathers by the prophets, has in these last days spoken to us by His Son.

As several savior characters (other than Jesus of Nazareth) are revealed it is imperative that we be mindful of two things:

1) God has spoken (from eternity) into time or at *various* times and in *various* ways (*by the prophets or by various* vessels*)*. In fact, God is perpetually speaking. In others words, God can speak *to*, and *through*, *anyone* at *anytime*.

2) God *also* spoke (more recently) through Jesus. However, Jesus is not the only Messenger (or Messiah) that God has sent, used or spoken to and through.

The Savior characters whom we will now research are not presented in any way with the intention of causing a crisis of faith, to diminish the Finished Work of the Cross, or to sway anyone away from their Christian (or Jesus centered) expression of worship. To be clear, I personally believe Jesus of Nazareth was a real person who walked the earth. I believe His miracles were real. I believe the crucifixion, resurrection and ascension were and are real. And, I love Jesus with all my heart, mind and strength. However, if hypothetically, the story of Jesus were a compilation of several different historical savior figures, it would in no way tarnish the beauty eternally contained in the idea of being reconnected to God by God incarnating in the human form of a selfless sacrifice or as an innocent Lamb.

These ancient and historical Saviors are merely presented in the hopes of enlarging our paradigm of the Christ. And, to embark on a new paradigm of the Christ that is bigger than any one specific Savior, yet present in them all.

The ancient Messianic figures who we will present are *Horus of Egypt, Mithras of Mesopotamia, and Krishna of India.* They all are remarkably similar to Jesus of Nazareth (in pedigree and in experience) and they all predate Jesus of Nazareth (3 of the 4 predate Jesus by one thousand years or more).

There is quite a bit of skepticism from some fundamentalist Christian circles regarding the accuracy of some of the facts related to these ancient savior characters. My desire is not to win an argument that only widens the chasm between progressive and evangelical Christians. Again, the impetus for this exercise is only to expose the truth of the eternal existence of the Christ in all of creation! Allow me to say that if only one half, or even one third, of these similarities are even fairly accurate, then there is justifiable cause to at least ponder the possibility that God has been sending the same message of truth, love and mercy to humanity throughout the ages in different geographical places to different cultures, peoples and languages using different messengers and saviors in an undying effort to reconnect with us. This information only sheds a light on the lengths to which God will go to in order to reach and redeem His creation.

HORUS of Egypt (around 3000 BC):

> ➢ Born of a virgin
> ➢ Only begotten son of the God Osiris

- Mother was Isis-Meri (Meriam or "Mary")
- Father named Seb (a.k.a. Jo-Seph)
- Of royal descent (Jesus, son of David the King)
- Birth was heralded by an angel to Isis, his mother
- The star Sirius, the morning star, shone over His birthplace
- Shepherds gathered at the place of His birth
- Herut (or Herod) tried to have Horus murdered
- God tells Horus' mother "Come, thou goddess Isis, hide thyself with thy child" (interesting to note that Jesus was hidden in Egypt to avoid being murdered as a baby)

- There is no data on Horus between ages of 12-30 (also no information on Jesus between the ages of 13-30)
- Horus began His ministry at age 30
- Horus was baptized in water at the river Eridanus
- He was baptized by Anup "the Baptizer" (Jesus was baptized by John "the Baptist")
- Anup "the Baptizer" was later beheaded (as was John the Baptist)
- He was taken from the desert of Amenta up a high mountain by his arch-rival Sut (Jesus taken from desert to a high mountain to be tempted by the devil)
- Sut was a precursor for the Hebrew Satan
- Horus resists the temptation of Sut

- He had twelve disciples
- Horus walked on water, cast out demons, healed the sick, restored sight to the blind
- He "stilled the sea by his power"
- Horus raised El-Osirus (or Lazarus) from the grave
- He preached His most famous sermon on a mountain
- This sermon was known as the "Sermon on the Mount"
- Horus died by way of crucifixion
- He died along side two thieves
- Horus was then placed in a tomb
- He descended into Hell

- And, resurrected after three days
- It was prophesied that, in the future, Horus would return to reign for 1,000 years in the Millennium

- Horus' ministry was supported mainly by women
- Horus was known as the "Savior of humanity," and as the "God-man"
- He carried the title "the anointed one" (or the Christ)
- He was also called the "good shepherd," the "lamb of God," the "bread of life," the "son of man" and "the Word"
- Astrologically, Horus is associated with Pisces, the fish (as is Jesus)
- Symbols that were used to denote Horus were the Fish, the vine and the shepherd's crook

- Horus gave criteria for receiving salvation and avoiding judgment: *I have given bread to the hungry man and water to the thirsty man and clothing to the naked person and a boat to the shipwrecked mariner* (also taught by Jesus in Matthew 25)

- Horus made several *I AM* statements: *I am Horus in glory...I am the Lord of Light...I am the victorious one...I am the heir of endless time...I, even I, am he that knoweth the paths of heaven*
- *I am Horus, the Prince of Eternity*
- *I am Horus who stepeth onward through eternity...eternity and everlastingness is my name*
- *I am the possessor of bread in Anu. I have bread in heaven with Ra*

MITHRA(S) of Mesopotamia, Babylon, Rome (earliest evidence dates to the Mid-First Century BC):

- ➤ Born of a virgin on December 25th
- ➤ Had twelve Disciples
- ➤ Was called The Good Shepherd; The Way, the Truth and the Light; Redeemer; Savior; Messiah; and was identified with the lion and the lamb

- ➤ The ceremonies in the Mithraic religion included a sort of baptism to remove sins, anointing, and a sacred meal of bread, accompanied by a consecrated wine believed to possess wonderful power (In the 2nd Century AD, Justin Martyr actually accused the Mithraic religion of copying the Christian Communion rite)

- ➤ Mithra was buried in a tomb and after three days he rose again
- ➤ His resurrection was celebrated every year
- ➤ It is interesting to note that the Vatican is built on the grounds previously devoted to the worship of Mithra (60 BC)

KRISHNA of India (3228 BC):

Most Christians, who are even cognizant of the similarities between Jesus and Krishna, have usually responded in three general ways:

1) Legends of Krishna's life are lies which Satan created to discredit Christianity in advance of Jesus' birth.

2) The similarities in the two lives are simple coincidences.

3) Krishna's life was a type of prophecy foretelling the arrival of the Christian Messiah.

Whatever opinion you may presently hold, the historical similarities between the Christian savior Jesus, and the Indian messiah Krishna, number in the hundreds. It should be noted that an earlier common English spelling of Krishna was "Christ-na," which reveals its relation to "Christ." Also, in Bengali, Krishna is reputedly "Christos," which is the same as the Greek for "Christ."

➤ Krishna was born of the Virgin Devaki ("Divine One") on December 25

➤ His birth was signaled by a star in the east and attended by angels and shepherds

➤ When they arrived, they presented Him with spices

➤ He was persecuted by a tyrant who ordered the slaughter of thousands of infants

➤ His earthly father was a carpenter (as was Joseph – Jesus' father)

➤ Krishna is the second person of the Hindu Trinity (as is Jesus – "Father, Son, Holy Spirit)

➤ He is depicted as having his foot on the head of a serpent

➤ His disciples purportedly bestowed upon him the title "Jezeus," or "Jeseus," meaning "pure essence"

➤ He was deemed the "Son of God" and "our Lord and Savior," who came to earth in order to die for man's salvation

➤ Krishna is the "lion of the tribe of Saki"

➤ He was called the "Shepherd of God" and considered the "Redeemer," "Firstborn," "Sin-Bearer," "Liberator," "Universal Word"

➤ Krishna was anointed on the head with oil by a woman whom he healed (as Jesus was by Mary Magdalene)

➤ He worked miracles and wonders, raising the dead and healing lepers, the deaf and the blind

➤ Krishna used parables to teach the people about charity and love, and he "lived poor and he loved the poor"

> He castigated the clergy, charging them with "ambition and hypocrisy . . . tradition says he fell victim to their vengeance"

> Krishna's "beloved disciple" was Arjuina or Ar-jouan (Jesus had John "the Beloved")
> He was transfigured in front of his disciples
> He gave his disciples the ability to work miracles
> In some traditions he died on a tree or was crucified between two thieves
> Krishna was killed around the age of 30, and the sun darkened at his death
> He rose from the dead and ascended to heaven "in the sight of all men"
> He was depicted on a cross with nail-holes in his feet

> Krishna is to return to judge the dead, riding on a white horse, and to do battle with the "Prince of Evil," who will desolate the earth

…Now, take a deep breath and let us try to assimilate what we have been presented.

There are several ways in which we can respond to this information:

1) We can refute it and say there are absolutely no correlations or similarities.

2) We can be shaken to the point that we lose faith.

3) We can feel like someone is attacking us and "our Jesus."

4) We can be fearful that we have now "Gone after other gods" and are somehow being unfaithful to Jesus.

5) Or we can look deeply enough to see that in God's love, mercy and desire to reconnect with humanity throughout history, God has providentially sent several Messengers with similar messages to show us The Way, and the way back to love and connection with our Divine Source!

Consider and apply Solomon's wisdom regarding the fallacy of NEW TRUTH, or even NEW TRUTH CARRIERS, in mankind's history:

WHAT HAS BEEN WILL BE AGAIN, WHAT HAS BEEN DONE WILL BE DONE AGAIN; THERE IS NOTHING NEW UNDER THE SUN. Is there anything of which one can say, "Look! This is something new"? IT WAS ALREADY HERE, LONG AGO; it was here before our time. THERE IS NO REMEMBRANCE OF MEN OF OLD, and even those who are yet to come will not be remembered by those who follow.
Ecclesiastes 1:9-11 NIV

That which is now HAS ALREADY BEEN, and that which is to be ALREADY HAS BEEN; and God seeks that which has passed by [SO THAT HISTORY REPEATS ITSELF].
Ecclesiastes 3:15 - AMP

In other words, Solomon proclaims everything that is, or ever will be, *has already been* and has always been (the Christ in Horus, Mithra, Krishna, Melchizedek and Jesus is, and always has been present in the earth). And, why does history inevitably continue to *repeat itself*? This cyclical phenomenon is evidence of the providential mercy of God and proof, if you will, that God continually sends Messengers (Messiahs) throughout history in an undying attempt to awaken mankind to the Divine. Solomon also adds that we will not remember the *men of old*; i.e. the followers of the savior Horus will not remember the savior Krishna; the followers of Mithra will not remember the Christ figure Melchizedek; and the followers of Jesus seem to refute that there has ever been any other Christ or savior figure except *their* Jesus. As long as we cling to our generation's savior figure to the exclusion of all others we fail to see the One God who sends the same message to each generation.

So, where do we go from here?

After coming into contact with information that could possibly serve to bridge the many chasms that separate religions, we must make a conscious decision to *never again* allow the religious ego (or the need to be right and therefore convert others to our way of thinking) to be a barrier that keeps spiritual people apart. Furthermore, as we choose to see the Christ throughout history, and in several different Messianic figures, we don't have to lose our connection to the Jesus Person in order to begin walking in the Christ Consciousness!

THE MYSTERY OF MELCHIZEDEK "THE CHRIST"

It is completely understandable that it may be somewhat difficult (at least for many Bible centered Christians) to seriously consider the information we have discussed in the section *Avatars and Other Incarnations of the Christ*. After all, Horus, Mithra, and Krishna cannot be found in the Bible.

But, WHAT IF WE UNCOVERED A CHRIST FIGURE, OTHER THAN JESUS OF NAZARETH, IN THE BIBLE? Such a figure exists. **Melchizedek, King of Salem and High Priest of the Most High God, is such a figure!** And, the truth of Melchizedek is easily found in the Bible when we open our minds, set our hearts to study the scriptures and decide to go beyond what lies on the surface.

Melchizedek has a presence in the Old Testament, but not nearly as often as He does in the New Testament. However, what we do find regarding Melchizedek in the Old Testament is quite significant. We discover that Abraham had an encounter with this priestly king of Salem, where he bestowed a blessing upon Abraham (or Abram). Later, we learn that Abraham gave a tenth (or a tithe) of all he had to Melchizedek. This tithe was the first of this type of financial pattern in the Judaic tradition.

The next mention of Melchizedek is from David who refers to Him as the father or priest of an *ORDER*. We also read that those who become a priest for God are actually becoming a part of this *ORDER OF MELCHIZEDEK... FOREVER*!

Then Melchizedek king of Salem brought out bread and wine; he was the priest of God Most High. And he blessed him and said: " Blessed be Abram of God Most High, Possessor of heaven and earth;

*And blessed be God Most High, Who has delivered
your enemies into your hand."*
Genesis 14:18-20 NKJV

*The LORD has sworn And will not relent, "You are a priest
FOREVER According to the order of Melchizedek."*
Psalm 110:4 - NKJV

As we research Melchizedek in the New testament we begin to
uncover irrefutable evidence and sufficient reason to believe that
Melchizedek was a type of Christ, or a Christ figure, who existed
in history long before the birth of Jesus of Nazareth. The book
of Genesis was written by Moses, somewhere around 1440 BC.
Yet, Abraham and Melchizedek (whom Moses is writing about in
Genesis 14) lived many generations before Moses. So, we know
that Melchizedek lived at least 1500 or more years before the birth
of Jesus.

*And it is yet far more evident if, IN THE LIKENESS OF
MELCHIZEDEK, there arises ANOTHER PRIEST who has come,
not according to the law of a fleshly commandment, but according
to the power of an endless life. For He testifies: " You are a priest
forever According to the order of Melchizedek."*
Hebrews 7:15-17 NIV

Who is this *other priest* who *arises in the likeness of Melchizedek?*
Who is this priest who comes in the Spirit of grace, not in the *law
of a fleshly commandment?* Who is this priest who brings with Him
the *power of an endless life?* Who is a *Priest According to the Order
of Melchizedek forever?*

Jesus! Jesus comes to revolutionize the law and the commandment *(you've heard of old, but I say)*. Jesus brings with Him the *power of an endless life*. Jesus comes in the *likeness of Melchizedek*. And, Jesus is a *priest according to the order of Melchizedek forever!*

Concerning Jesus being in the likeness of Melchizedek we find the phrase *You are a priest According to the Order of Melchizedek forever* six times! (Psalm 110:4; Hebrews 5:6 & 10; Hebrews 6:20; Hebrews 7:11 & 17)

So, let us examine why Melchizedek is a Christ before Jesus was born.

For this Melchizedek, king of Salem, priest of the Most High God, who met Abraham returning from the slaughter of the kings and blessed him, to whom also Abraham gave a tenth part of all, first being translated KING OF RIGHTEOUSNESS, and then also king of Salem, meaning KING OF PEACE.
Hebrews 7:1-2 NKJV

Notice, Melchizedek is referred to as KING OF RIGHTEOUSNESS and KING OF PEACE (as was Jesus).

(Melchizedek is) WITHOUT FATHER, WITHOUT MOTHER, without genealogy, HAVING NEITHER BEGINNING OF DAYS NOR END OF LIFE, but MADE LIKE THE SON OF GOD, remains a priest continually.
Hebrews 7:3 NKJV

Wow! Verse 3 is full of revelation.

> First, Melchizedek has no earthly father or mother – but like Jesus – was conceived by the Holy Spirit or comes to earth without fleshly initiation.

> Melchizedek also has no *beginning of days* and no *end of life* (*Alpha and Omega* – just like Jesus).

> And finally, Melchizedek was *MADE LIKE THE SON OF GOD!*

Melchizedek is *made like the Son of God*. And, Jesus comes *in the likeness of Melchizedek* (the first biblical Christ)!

Jesus is not only the 2nd Adam, He is also possibly the 2nd Christ!

Now consider how great this man was, to whom even the patriarch Abraham gave a tenth of the spoils... Now beyond all contradiction the lesser is blessed by the better... Even Levi, who receives tithes, paid tithes through Abraham, so to speak, for he was still in the loins of his father when Melchizedek met him.
Hebrews 7:4, 7, 9-10 NKJV

Abraham, the *Father of the faithful*, sensed the Christ in Melchizedek so strongly that he gave him a tenth of everything (or a tithe). This passage goes on to add the *lesser* (Abraham) is blessed by the *better* (Melchizedek). This verse is referring to the blessing that Melchizedek bestowed upon Abraham (or Abram) in Genesis 14. So, Paul writes here that Melchizedek is even more highly esteemed than Father Abraham. Paul expresses that Melchizedek is worthy of so much honor that he actually received tithes generationally, as Levi (yet to be born) was paying tithe to Melchizedek - before he was ever conceived - through Abraham.

"The LORD has sworn And will not relent, ' You are a priest forever According to the order of Melchizedek,'" by so much more Jesus has become a surety of a better covenant. Also there were many priests, because they were prevented by death from continuing. But He, because He continues forever, has an unchangeable priesthood.
Hebrews 7:21-24 NKJV

Jesus, who is the continuation of the Priesthood and Order of Melchizedek, is said to have an unchangeable priesthood. So, Jesus comes to change, or at least to challenge, the *Levitical Priesthood*, but not to change the unchangeable *Melchizedek Priesthood*.

MELCHIZEDEK (1500 BC or earlier):

➤ Miraculous birth or conceived by the Spirit, not flesh (*without father or mother*)
➤ Melchizedek is Alpha and Omega – like Jesus (*no beginning of days or end of days*)
➤ Has the likeness of the Jesus Person to come (*made like the Son of God*)

➤ Called *King of Peace* and *King of Righteousness* (Jesus is the *Prince of Peace / Jesus Christ, the Righteous One* - I John 2:1)
➤ Melchizedek and Jesus are referred to as King and as High Priest

➤ Melchizedek is eternal and the *Order of Melchizedek* is *forever!*
➤ Melchizedek is referred to as having the *power of an endless life* (Jesus came to bring eternal life)

Interesting that in chapters 5 and 6 of Hebrews, where we discover information about Melchizedek, we find phrases like:

For though by this time you ought to be teachers, you need someone to teach you again the first principles of the oracles of God; and you have come to need milk and not solid food. For everyone who partakes only of milk is unskilled in the word of righteousness, for he is a babe. But solid food belongs to those who are of full age...
Hebrews 5:12-14 – NKJV

Therefore, leaving the discussion of the elementary principles of Christ, let us go on to perfection...
Hebrews 6:1 – NKJV

Paul is encouraging us to grow up and to grow in revelation, chastising us that we should be fully weaned from milk (or past the *elementary principles*) and that we should be teachers, not babes. It is almost as if Paul is preparing us for the revelation we are about to receive in chapter 7 of Hebrews!

I CAN'T BE JESUS…BUT I CAN BECOME THE CHRIST

There has only been one historical Jesus. Yet, the Christ has been in, and is in, many! We are the Christ – the Body of Christ. Or, at least we can become the Christ as we learn, and choose, to *take every thought into captivity*. One of the greatest enemies to us becoming the Christ is the notion that we are not worthy to carry the Spirit of the Christ within us.

And if the Spirit of him who raised Jesus from the dead is living in you, he who raised Christ from the dead will also give life to your mortal bodies through HIS SPIRIT, WHO LIVES IN YOU.
Romans 8:11 – NIV

The SPIRIT OF GOD, who raised Jesus from the dead, LIVES IN YOU. And just as God raised Christ Jesus from the dead, he will give life to your mortal bodies by this SAME SPIRIT LIVING WITHIN YOU.
Romans 8:11 – New Living

Notice that the Spirit that lived in Jesus now lives in us. The New Living Bible plainly says the *SAME SPIRIT* that was in Jesus is now *LIVING WITHIN YOU!* The Christ Spirit that lived within Jesus – lives within us. And, the more we accept and surrender to our god-likeness – the more we will be able to awaken the Christ in others. Jesus was so comfortable with this idea that he encourages the disciples to do *greater works* than He did *(John 14:12)*.

Consider these verses that reveal to us the truth that we all innately carry the image and likeness of Divinity:

*Then God said, "Let us make man in our image, in our likeness...
So God created man in his own image, in the image of God he
created him; male and female he created them.*
Genesis 1:26-27 NKJV

"I said, 'You are "gods"; you are all sons of the Most High.'
Psalm 82:6 NIV

*Jesus answered them, "Is it not written in your Law,
'I have said you are gods'?*
John 10:34 - NIV

*Therefore you shall be perfect, just as your
Father in heaven is perfect.*
Matthew 5:48 NKJV

*till we all come to the unity of the faith and of the knowledge of the
Son of God, to a perfect man, to the measure of the stature
of the fullness of Christ*
Ephesians 4:13 – NKJV

Notice that we must first come to the knowledge, but then we are to
become a perfect man, taking on the measure of the stature of the
fullness of Christ! Let us be aware that *it pleased the Father for the
fullness to dwell in Jesus (Colossians 1:19).* And, it also pleases the
Father for that same fullness to dwell in us.

*Love has been perfected among us in this: that we may have
boldness in the day of judgment; because as He is,
SO ARE WE in this world.*
I John 4:17 - NKJV

Love is perfected among us as we realize that *as He is...SO ARE WE!* Where there is fear, love has not yet been perfected. *Perfect love casts out fear (I John 4:18).* And when we wake up to the Christ within us, love will become perfected! After all, why would we fear the *day of judgment*? God will not banish Himself to an eternal hell.

Nevertheless when one turns to the Lord, the veil is taken away. Now the Lord is the Spirit; and where the Spirit of the Lord is, there is liberty. But we all, with unveiled face, BEHOLDING AS IN A MIRROR the glory of the Lord, are being transformed into the SAME IMAGE from glory to glory, just as by the Spirit of the Lord.
II Corinthians 3:16-18 NKJV

When the veil of flesh is finally removed – the glory of God is revealed. Where is the glory revealed? In the mirror! In our faces! We are being transformed into the SAME IMAGE as Christ!

To them God willed to make known what are the riches of the glory of this mystery among the Gentiles: which is CHRIST IN YOU, the hope of glory.
Colossians 1:27 - NKJV

Christ IN US...THROUGH US...and AS US...is the hope of glory.

When we see the Christ in ourselves, we will begin to see the Christ in others.

And, when we see the Christ in others, we will finally realize peace on earth.

The Holy Bible of Inclusion

Part VIII – GROWING AN INCLUSIVE CHURCH
(Wisdom for Inclusive-minded pastors)

———◆———

-PACE and SPACE-
✳

-TERMS and LITURGIES-
✳

-STRATEGIES FOR ENGAGING IN BIBLICAL DISCUSSION-
✳

-THE PROGRESSION OF TRUTH-
✳

PACE AND SPACE

Change is the only constant in this world.
Everything will change.
Everyone will change.
However, every person (and system) changes at their own *pace* and in their own *space*.

Some people will change less than others. Significant change for one person may be considered small or insignificant by another person. Yet, all change is important. It is all progress. And, all change is a struggle.

> *Where there is no Struggle there is no Progress.*
> **Frederick Douglass**

However, we must allow people, and specifically congregants, to struggle through change (or to consider new truth) at whatever speed they are comfortable, and in the way they deem appropriate for their own path toward greater and deeper truth. If we choose to ignore the truth of permitting change to happen for people at their own pace and in their own space, then we will do so at our own peril, and at the peril of the movement of Inclusion.

Contrary to popular opinion, and against overwhelming evidence and experience, it is possible to GROW AN INCLUSIVE CHURCH!

Be mindful that preachers, teachers, ministers and even devoted seekers will customarily and willingly spend their time reading the Bible and other books that stimulate progress and challenge paradigm. By the time I began to preach on the subject of Universal Salvation I had been considering, questioning and researching for myself for almost fifteen years.

One Sunday morning, as I opened my mouth to deliver what I thought would be an awe-inspiring sermon entitled, *Jesus, and the Christ*, I watched painfully as eyes widened with surprise and jaws dropped in disbelief, as many people in my congregation were hearing this idea for the very first time. After a season of unsuccessfully attempting to force-feed people this new truth that was amazing to me, I had to surrender to the fact that people will eventually change (or at least consider new and unfamiliar truth), but they will do so, and must be allowed to do so in their own time.

We must always remember that the truth burning in us, and finding a home within us, may be new to many people we encounter. So, when introducing a new truth it would be wise to use phrases like:

> ➤ Consider this…
> ➤ Can we entertain this question?
> ➤ Allow me to suggest…

If you find that you've force fed your sheep, or even your family or friends, don't be too proud to apologize and then start again at a pace that encourages people to think while still keeping them from abandoning progress altogether.

TERMS AND LITURGIES

TERMS...

People of different backgrounds may actually be speaking the same truth but because they are using different language and semantics they may perceive that their ideas are in conflict. As a church is becoming more inclusive there may be some new terms that are used to alert a larger audience (the whole household of God) that they are welcome. However, the long-term congregants may be unfamiliar – or even frightened – by these new terms. So be, and remain, conscious of this and always be willing to explain what you are saying in a variety of ways, especially if your audience is made up of people with diverse belief systems. In other words, as Paul encourages - *become all things to all people (I Corinthians 9).* As we become all things to the Buddhist and to the Muslim and to those who may be unawakened to the Christ, we must also remember to be all things to the Bible-based Christian who has for many years been a faithful member.

The phrase *THE WORLD IS SAVED* – should be explained to Christian audiences who have been longtime Evangelicals. Very simply explain that because of the Finished Work of Jesus at Calvary, the *world is now reconciled to God.* However, there are many who have not yet had their *minds* reconciled, although their *souls* have already been reconciled.

The term *CONSCIOUSNESS* – can be explained as *awareness.* Progressing in Consciousness is the journey toward a greater awareness and awakening, first of self, and then of truth.

The terms *ENERGY and VIBRATION* – are what Pentecostals or Charismatics might refer to as *anointing* or as the *Holy Ghost* or as the *Presence of God.*

The term *UNIVERSE* – is nothing more than a way of saying God (and is also a reference to the laws of God that govern all created things).

There are many other terms and phrases that may be unsettling to people who are only familiar with their own limited expression and vernacular, yet as architects of a movement, we must be constantly aware of any potential chasm that would try to separate people of like mind and heart.

Also, remember that if you use a quote from a holy book other than the Bible or teach a truth from a spiritual teacher or messenger other than Jesus, relate it to a similar truth from the Bible or to a teaching of Jesus. For instance, if you quote Buddha, find a similar teaching from the Bible to show that truth has no boundaries religious or otherwise:

➢ Buddha said - *Man is the sum total of his thoughts.* Similarly, the book of Proverbs teaches – *As a man thinks in his heart, so is he.*

➢ *Karma* is the Buddhist way of teaching *Sowing and Reaping* (taught by Jesus).

Also, show the similarities of different religions as a way to bridge the gaps dividing people groups:

➢ In Judaism, the Torah commands - *That which is hateful to you, do not do to your fellow.*

➢ In Islam, there is a hadith that reads - *None of you truly believes until he wishes for his brother what he wishes for himself.*

➢ Likewise, Jesus told us to - *love thy neighbor as thyself.*

Little illustrations like this help people to see a larger vision of God outside of their circle while allowing them to retain the security offered to them within their circle.

LITURGIES...

COMMUNION – is probably the most common and considered the most sacred liturgy of the Christian church. As we walk into a more inclusive paradigm we need not lose this ancient expression of worship. Yet, we do need to redefine the elements. It was once taught to us that the *Bread* (or *Body of Jesus*) represented the breaking of the Body of Jesus as a substitutionary sacrifice for us. While this is not necessarily wrong, we can add more depth and beauty to this limited description. We must now receive the bread IN REMEMBRANCE of the Christ, re-membering (or putting back together) the Universal Body of the Christ, not just an exclusive re-gathering of Christians only. This sacred moment of remembrance should be utilized as an opportunity to teach the need for interfaith tolerance, celebration and even Oneness. When we receive the *Wine* (or the *Blood of Jesus*) we must first and foremost be conscious that *God did not kill Jesus* so that He could love us. To be clear, no one killed Jesus, He willingly laid down His life. Also, God does not kill in order to love. God IS Love. Love is the essence, or IS-ness of God not the action, reaction or response of God. So, the blood in communion should now represent the lengths to which Jesus was willing to go to in order to reconnect us in consciousness to God. We must always be mindful that God did not kill Jesus so that He could love us. Jesus shed His blood to reconnect us to God in consciousness! Let us set our intention to always have communion as part of our liturgy. It is beautiful, sacred and deeper than we have ever known.

WATER BAPTISM – has been thought of as necessary for salvation (*unless you are born of water and Spirit you will not enter the kingdom - John 3:5*). Being *born of water and of Spirit* stands in contrast to being stuck in the law or in literalism. The actual water holds no magical power. The power is in the mind that perceives the love of God. Water baptism does not save us, but it can be a powerful way for a person to publicly recognize that he has been reconciled. The water now becomes symbolic of our transition from *flesh* to *Spirit*. As we are immersed in the water, the flesh mind that perceives separation from God is dying. As we emerge from the water we are reborn into the new consciousness that we are one with God.

ALTAR CALLS – are the traditional way to end most Evangelical church services (the invitation given to sinners to come forward and make Jesus your personal Lord and Savior). This liturgy of the Christian Church has been so meaningful for people that many actually remember the exact date that they responded to an invitation for salvation by willfully walking down an aisle. It is not necessary to omit this expression as we become more inclusive. However, the fear driven invitation, "If you were to die tonight…would you spend eternity in heaven or hell" needs a little work as we have now come to the knowledge that the Second Adam is greater than the First Adam; that hell has been conquered; and the price of sin has been paid. Whereas we believe that the world is, and has been, reconciled to God through the finished work of Christ (II Corinthians 5) we now invite people to come to the altar, not so much to get saved but to recognize or awaken to the salvation that is already theirs, purchased *from the foundation of the world*. A friend of mine invites people to the altar this way, "God has made peace with you through the Christ, but you may need to come and make your peace with God." Thus, altar calls are not about getting saved, but about recognizing salvation.

As the traditional Christian church makes the decision to become more inclusive, we must also set our intention to not remove the liturgies and pillars of our worship. They need not be removed... only redefined! Keeping these familiar and sacred elements of worship will help to grow an inclusive church.

STRATEGY FOR ENGAGING IN BIBLICAL DISCUSSION

We must focus not only on growing a more inclusive local church, but also on creating a more inclusive expression for the Universal Body of Christ by encouraging civil discussion between Christians who may not interpret scripture the same way. Some philosophers have noted that to *agree to disagree* is actually the highest form of agreement.

Allow me to offer 4 simple suggestions that encourage theological discussion while also promoting and salvaging unity.

1) Realize that Christ is ONE...but MANY members

For I say, through the grace given to me, to everyone who is among you, not to think of himself more highly than he ought to think, but to think soberly, as God has dealt to each one a measure of faith. For as we have many members in one body, but all the members do not have the same function, so we, being many, are one body in Christ, and individually members of one another. Having then gifts differing according to the grace that is given to us, let us use them... Be of the same mind toward one another. Do not set your mind on high things, but associate with the humble. Do not be wise in your own opinion. Repay no one evil for evil. Have regard for good things in the sight of all men. If it is possible, as much as depends on you, live peaceably with all men.
Romans 12:3-6, 16-18 -NKJV

For as the body is one and has many members, but all the members of that one body, being many, are one body, so also is Christ. For by one Spirit we were all baptized into one body—

284

whether Jews or Greeks, whether slaves or free—and have all been made to drink into one Spirit. For in fact the body is not one member but many. But God composed the body, having given greater honor to that part which lacks it, that there should be no schism in the body, but that the members should have the same care for one another. And if one member suffers, all the members suffer with it; or if one member is honored, all the members rejoice with it.
Now you are the body of Christ, and members individually.
I Corinthians 12:12-14, 25-27 - NKJV

2) Remember that ALL of the members support the work of the Christ

There is one body and one Spirit, just as you were called in one hope of your calling; one Lord, one faith, one baptism; one God and Father of all, who is above all, and through all, and in you all... from whom the whole body, joined and knit together by what every joint supplies, according to the effective working by which every part does its share, causes growth of the body for the edifying of itself in love. Therefore, putting away lying, " Let each one of you speak truth with his neighbor," for we are members of one another. "Be angry, and do not sin": do not let the sun go down on your wrath, nor give place to the devil.
Ephesians 4:4-6, 16, 25-27 - NKJV

3) Let us AGREE that Argument is counterproductive

Agree with your adversary quickly, while you are on the way with him
Matthew 5:25 – NKJV

"Come now, let us reason together," says the LORD. "Though your sins are like scarlet, they shall be as white as snow; though they are red as crimson, they shall be like wool.
Isaiah 1:18 – NKJV

4) Be Ready to GIVE AN ANSWER (with gentleness and respect)

Who is going to harm you if you are eager to do good? But even if you should suffer for what is right, you are blessed. "Do not fear their threats; do not be frightened." But in your hearts revere Christ as Lord. Always be prepared to GIVE AN ANSWER to everyone who asks you to give the reason for the hope that you have. But do this with gentleness and respect, keeping a clear conscience, so that those who speak maliciously against your good behavior in Christ may be ashamed of their slander. For it is better, if it is God's will, to suffer for doing good than for doing evil. For Christ also suffered once for sins, the righteous for the unrighteous, to bring you to God.
I Peter 3:13-18 NIV

THE PROGRESSION OF TRUTH

Let me now reiterate what I stated in the earlier section, *The Eternal Christ*. For now we live in TIME. However, God lives in ETERNITY. God, who is simultaneously the *alpha and omega, beginning and end, first and last*, even *declaring the end from the beginning*, is more like a continuous eternal-cycle or eternal-circle than a time-line. So, in order to catch a glimpse into the ETERNAL MIND of God we must think outside the confines of time and past the boundaries of time-lines. We must think spherically, not linearly. And, we must welcome eternity into our limited time-space understanding.

A circle (or cycle), like eternity, is unending. Many things in nature reflect this circular, cyclical pattern. The seasons change in succession and then repeat themselves year after year; seed time and harvest, the water cycle, the planets as they orbit the sun. All plant life is born, flourishes and flowers, withers and dies, shedding seeds that drop in the ground to be born again.

Observant students of history have noticed a very specific cycle. According to Ralph Adams Cram, author of a work written in 1908 entitled *The Great Thousand Years*, as rhythmic as the human heart beat are these "five hundred year epochs, a tide that rises and falls in obedience to some primal and unknowable law, signalized in its tremendous beatings by the lives of men who are instruments of the Will of God . . ."

The following is a list ranging from 1500 years prior to the birth of Jesus to 2000 years afterward showing very clearly the pattern in approximately five hundred year intervals where there seems to be a fresh awakening, and a new allowance, for truth to break through the barriers of traditionalism, fundamentalism and literalism.

➢ 1500 B.C. – The Vedas (oldest Hindu sacred texts) were begun

➢ 1000 B.C. – (Judaism) David becomes King of Israel, establishing the beginning of the lineage the House of David, which every subsequent king (as well as Jesus of Nazareth) in both the ancient Kingdom of Israel and the later Kingdom of Judah, traced their heritage from in order to validate their right to rule Israel. The Kingdom of David symbolized a new openness and was an *inclusive* kingdom that encouraged all of Israel to enter and worship in the temple (in contrast with the Kingdom of Saul that limited temple worship to an exclusive group)

➢ 563 B.C. - The birth of Siddhartha Gautama, The Buddha (the "awakened one" or "enlightened one")

➢ 30 A.D. – Jesus the Christ challenges the long held views of Judaism (also around the 1st century A.D. early church fathers Origen, Clement of Alexandria, Gregory of Nyssa and others taught the doctrine of Universal Salvation)

➢ 500 A.D. – A theologian named Pelagius denies the doctrine of original sin and teaches of the good nature of humanity in sharp contrast to St. Augustine

➢ 1000 A.D. – Islam experiences a Golden Age, leading the world's economy as well as introducing the scientific method (which is still used today)

➢ 1517 A.D. – Martin Luther nails his 95 theses to the door of Castle Church in Wittenberg, Germany, beginning the Protestant Reformation

➤ 2012 A.D. – In the Precession of Equinoxes, the Age of Pisces (which began roughly with the birth of Jesus and saw the rise of most major monotheistic religions) gives way to the dawning of the Age of Aquarius (the age when everything becomes unified)

Truth does not belong to any one person, group or even era. Eternal truth seems to find its way into time through the hearts of willing individuals who are surrendered to let truth flow to and then through them. Every person has a certain capacity for truth. Those who seem to be enlightened (or those who have changed the landscape of history) are actually no wiser or any more spiritual than any one else. We have every bit as much potential as did Jesus, Paul, Martin Luther King, Jr., or Gandhi. The enlightened have merely learned how to clear out enough space for truth to be housed within them.

In the Genesis account of creation this is precisely what we find. In the very first verse of the Bible we find the words, *In the beginning God created*. The word *created* in Hebrew is *bara* – meaning to *clear out*. In other words, creation is a process of finding or allotting enough unoccupied space for God to have room to work. Creation is always happening in those who have cleared out enough space for it to be facilitated.

The Old Testament prophet Elijah once encountered a widow who was in dire need. He instructed the widow to go and gather *empty vessels*. As she gathered emptiness, the Bible records that a mysterious oil flowed and continued to flow. Yet, when all the vessels were full, the oil ceased to flow. Truth, revelation and wisdom continue to flow as long as there is an empty vessel and enough space to accommodate it. In other words, as long as we remain open and refuse to act as if we know it all, truth will continue to flow to and through us. Jesus confirms this idea by encouraging us to ask, seek and knock – and to *KEEP ON* asking and seeking and knocking.

So I say to you, Ask and KEEP ON asking and it shall be given you; seek and KEEP ON seeking and you shall find; knock and KEEP ON knocking and the door shall be opened to you.
Luke 11:9 - Amplified

In other words, once you find one truth, don't quit searching for more. KEEP ON!

It is impossible to conceive when we have preconceived. When we decide to keep an open mind we send the only invitation that truth awaits. As we find this delicate balance of flowing in fresh truth the temptation will arise to believe that we are receiving new truth.

There is no new truth.

Truth never changes.

Our idea of God is simply getting better with time and with openness.

Truth never changes, but what we have to deal with on this plane is man's apprehension of the Truth, and, throughout historical time, this has been steadily and continuously improving. In fact, what we call progress is but the outer expression corresponding to mankind's continuously improving idea of God.
Emmet Fox – Sermon On The Mount

Truth is revealed to us in a progression, and the amount of truth we receive at any given time is in direct proportion to how much unoccupied space (religious, spiritual, mental, intellectual) we choose to maintain. This pattern of thinking assures us that truth will never be a stranger but will continue to find its way to us *line upon line, precept upon precept, here a little, there a little (Isaiah 28:10, 13 NKJV).*

Whether we cite the example of Jesus growing from being only the savior of the *lost sheep of the house of Israel* into the *Christ, savior of the world*; or if we explore the Apostle Paul's progression of truth regarding receiving salvation only by *belief* and *confession (Romans 10:9-10 NKJV)* to the revelation that *Christ is all and is in all (Colossians 3:11 NKJV)* what we find is that even the most enlightened continuously grow into higher truths and deeper revelations. This allowance for constant transformation is actually a sure sign that enlightenment is happening.

As Solomon teaches, *there is nothing new under the sun* and *that which is* or ever will be *has already been before.* Applying this wisdom to our theological endeavors would simply mean that there really are no new truths, only ancient and eternal truths waiting to be uncovered, or recovered. So, when truth is revealed to us we must realize that someone, somewhere, at some time has already sensed and seen it before us. This is also a humbling thought when we realize that we do not possess a monopoly on truth nor do we hold a corner on truth.

> *Do not conform any longer to the pattern of this world,*
> *but be transformed by the RENEWING of your mind.*
> **Romans 12:2 NIV**

We are not transformed by the renewed mind, but by the mind that is perpetually *RENEWING* or even re-knowing. Jesus, Paul, Billy Graham and others are not known (or remembered) for stagnation. They will be heralded throughout history as those who had a dynamic grasp of revelation. They will be remembered for their bold and cutting edge truths. And, to the observant reader, these men will be celebrated because they were willing to journey from one plateau of truth to even higher ones in their own generation. These men were not reformed theologians, but rather ever reforming thinkers.

When we choose to honor truth by allowing it to progress to us, in us, through us and eventually as us, we will discover a path that will continue to present us with fresh truth for a lifetime.